Mutagenic Monsters

Written, designed, and created by Alex Visintainer

Introduction

Welcome to Mutagenic Monsters! This is not only a coloring book but also a beastiary of all the wild creatures that exist in my imagination. I captured them all on the pages for you readers to color and give life to. It'd be no fun just giving you all the details of each of these monsters so I am tasking you with making up your own details about them. Let your imagination flow as you travel through the land of these Mutagenic Monsters!!!!!

Instructions Page:

On this book safari, every page has a blank monster report to the left of the picture. It's your duty as the adventurer to fill these out to complete the beastiary and educate others about these monsters. Use your imagination and practice creativity to bring life to these creatures. There are no wrong answers so don't hold back!

WARNING!!!!!
BEWARE OF THE
MUTAGENIC MONSTERS
AHEAD!!!!!

MONSTER REPORT

Monster Name:_____

Originates From:_____

Diet:_____

Description:_____

_____

_____

_____

_____

_____

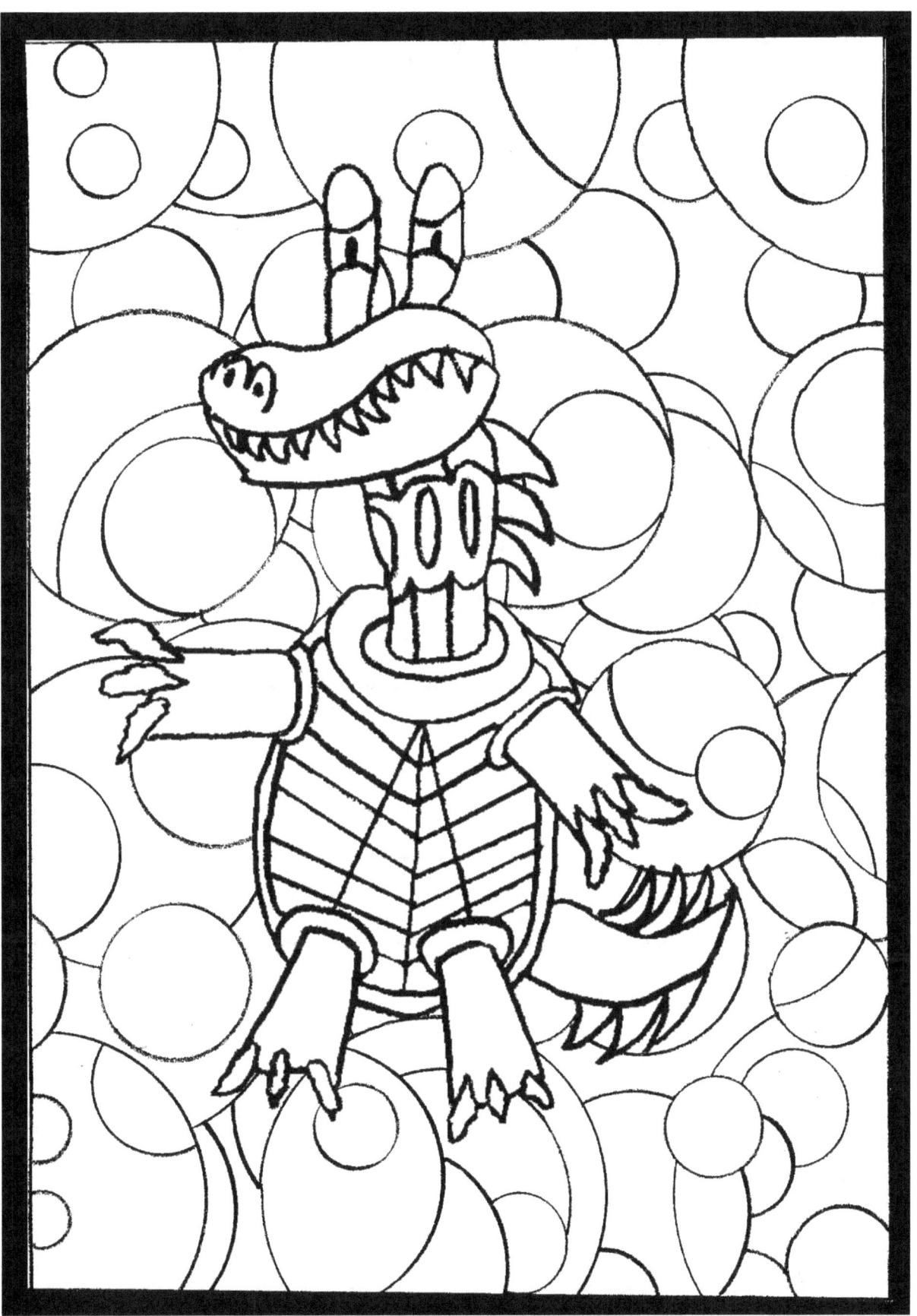

MONSTER REPORT

Monster Name:_____

Originates From:_____

Diet:_____

Description:_____

_____

_____

_____

_____

_____

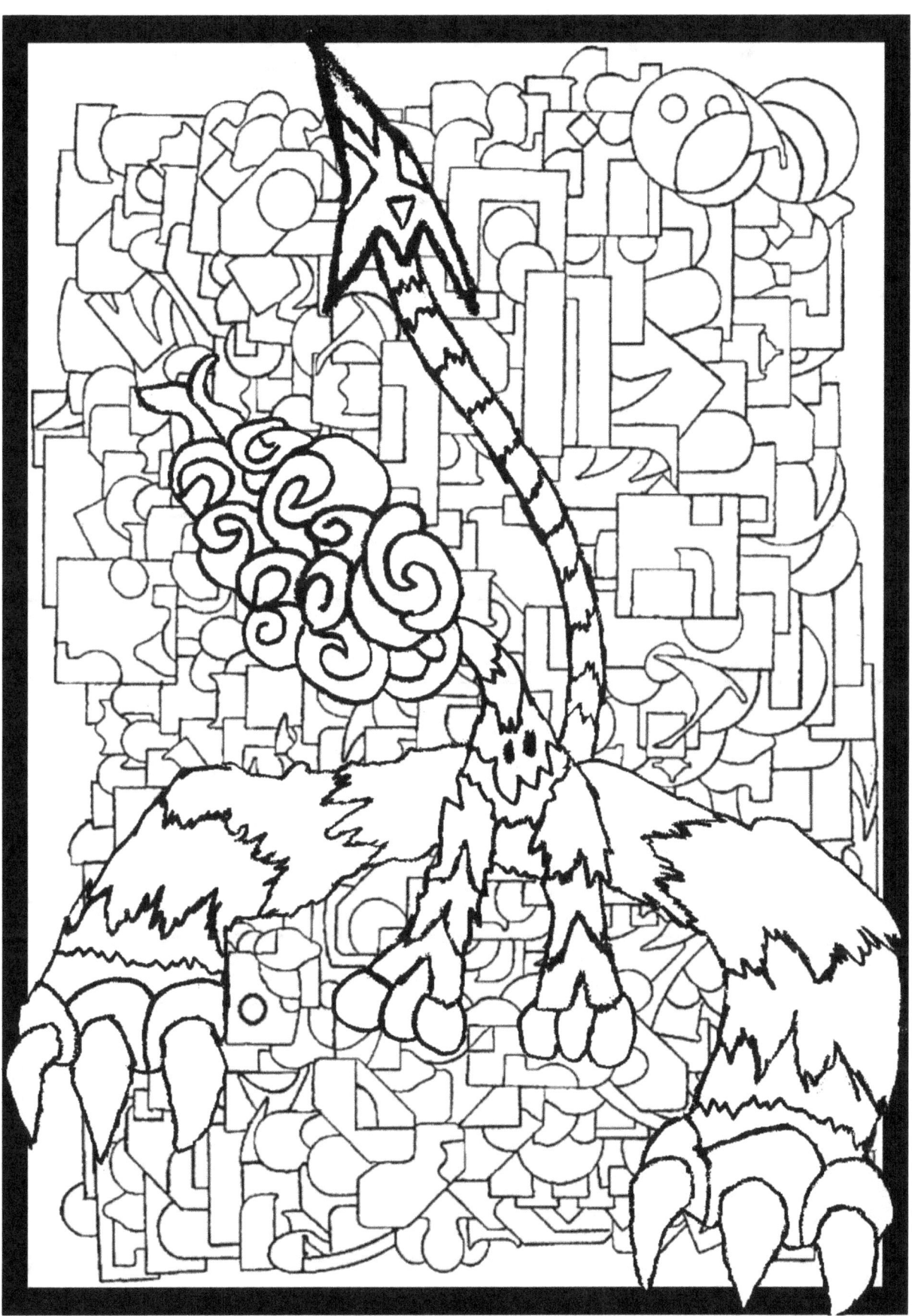

MONSTER REPORT

Monster Name:_____

Originates From:_____

Diet:_____

Description:_____

_____

_____

_____

_____

_____

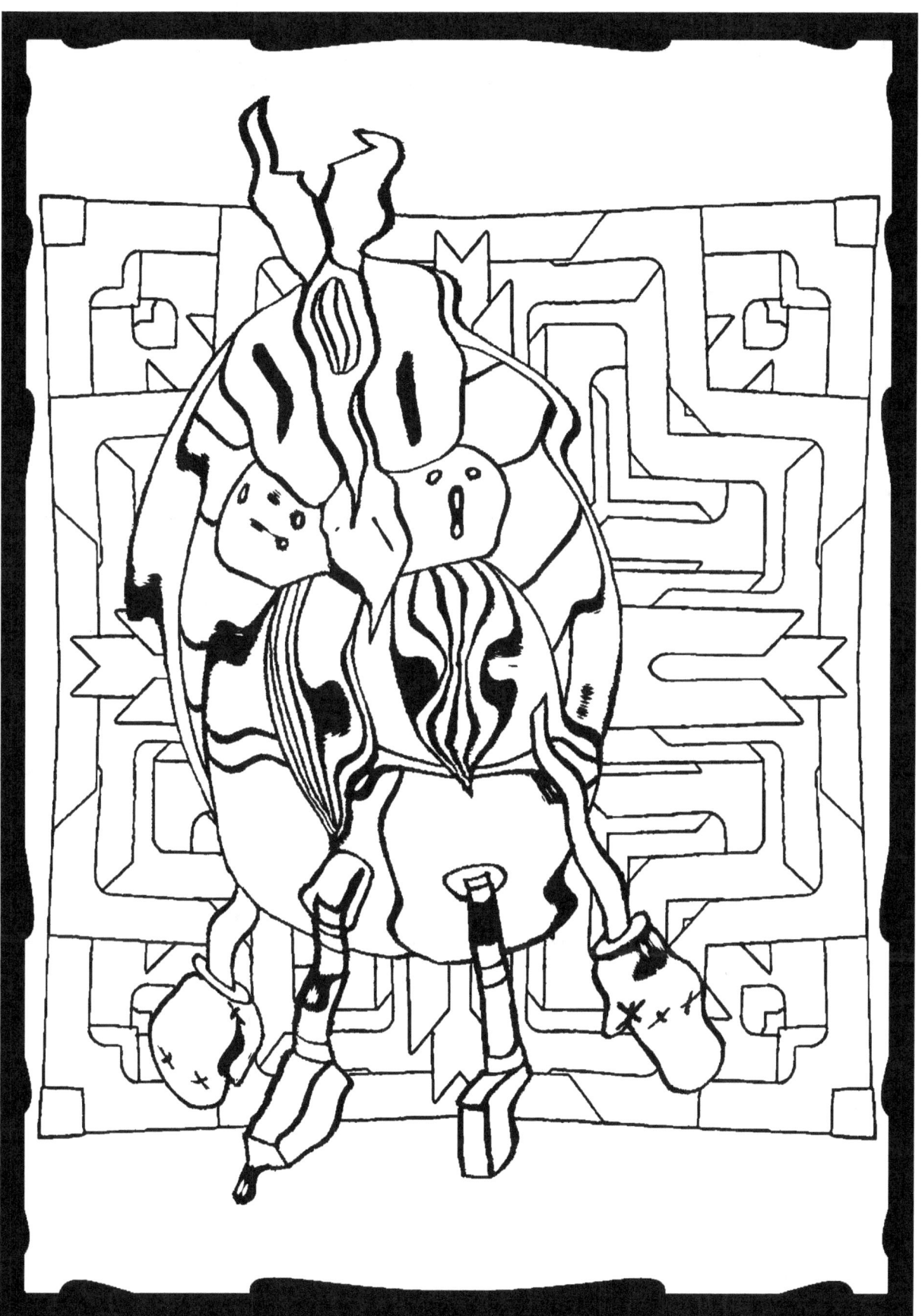

MONSTER REPORT

Monster Name:_____

Originates From:_____

Diet:_____

Description:_____

_____

_____

_____

_____

_____

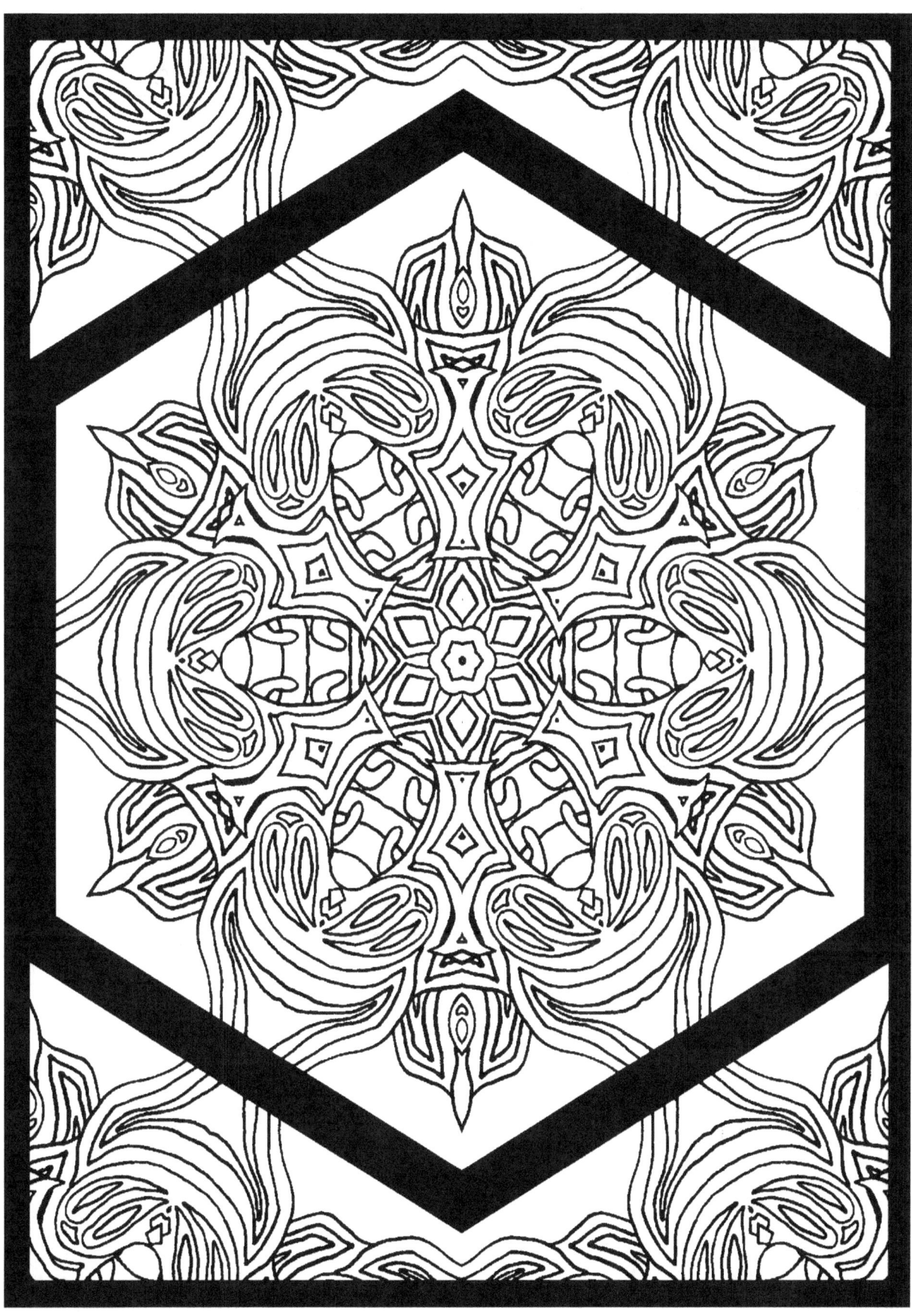

MONSTER REPORT

Monster Name:_____

Originates From:_____

Diet:_____

Description:_____

_____

_____

_____

_____

_____

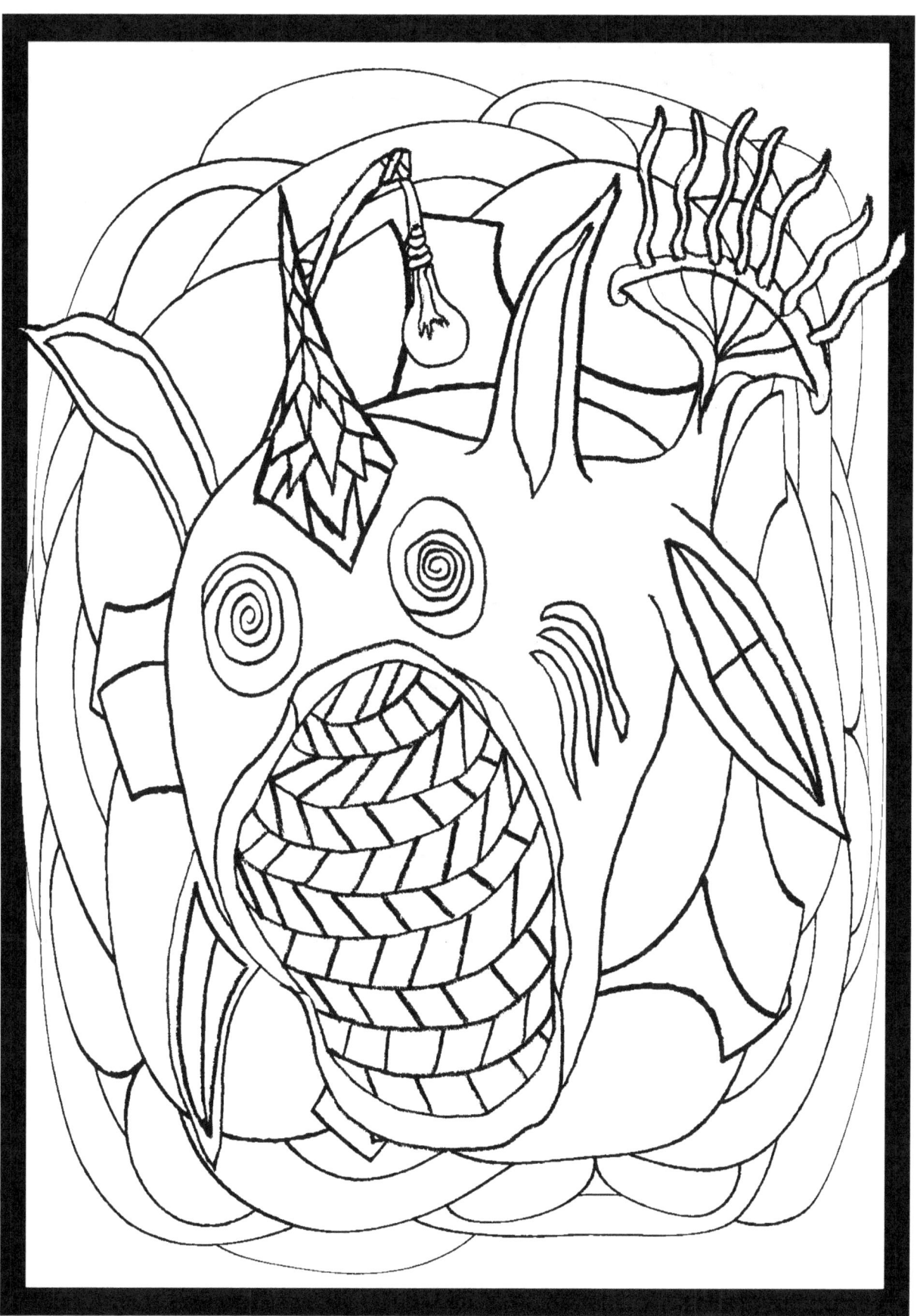

MONSTER REPORT

Monster Name:_____

Originates From:_____

Diet:_____

Description:_____

_____

_____

_____

_____

_____

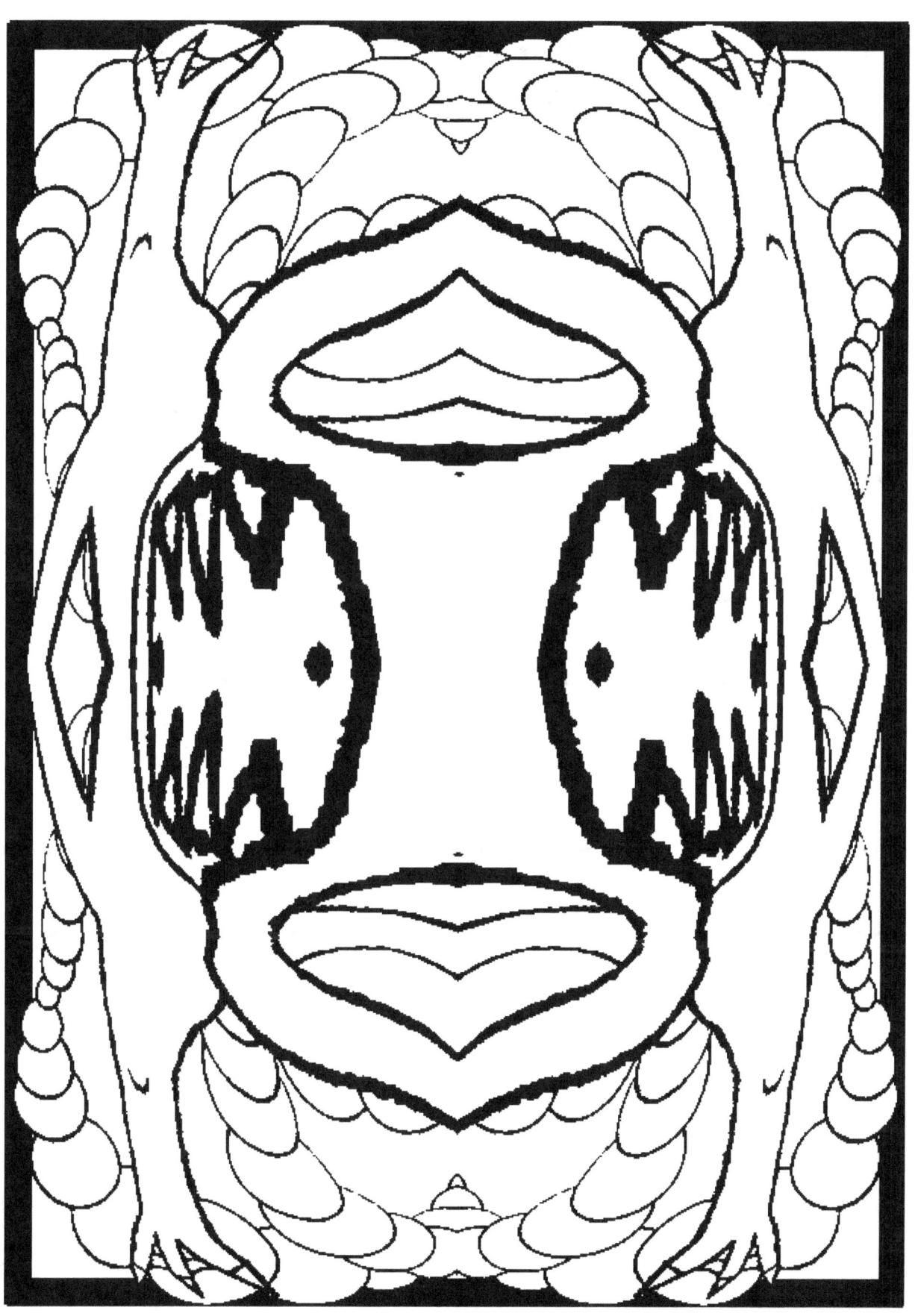

MONSTER REPORT

Monster Name:_____

Originates From:_____

Diet:_____

Description:_____

_____

_____

_____

_____

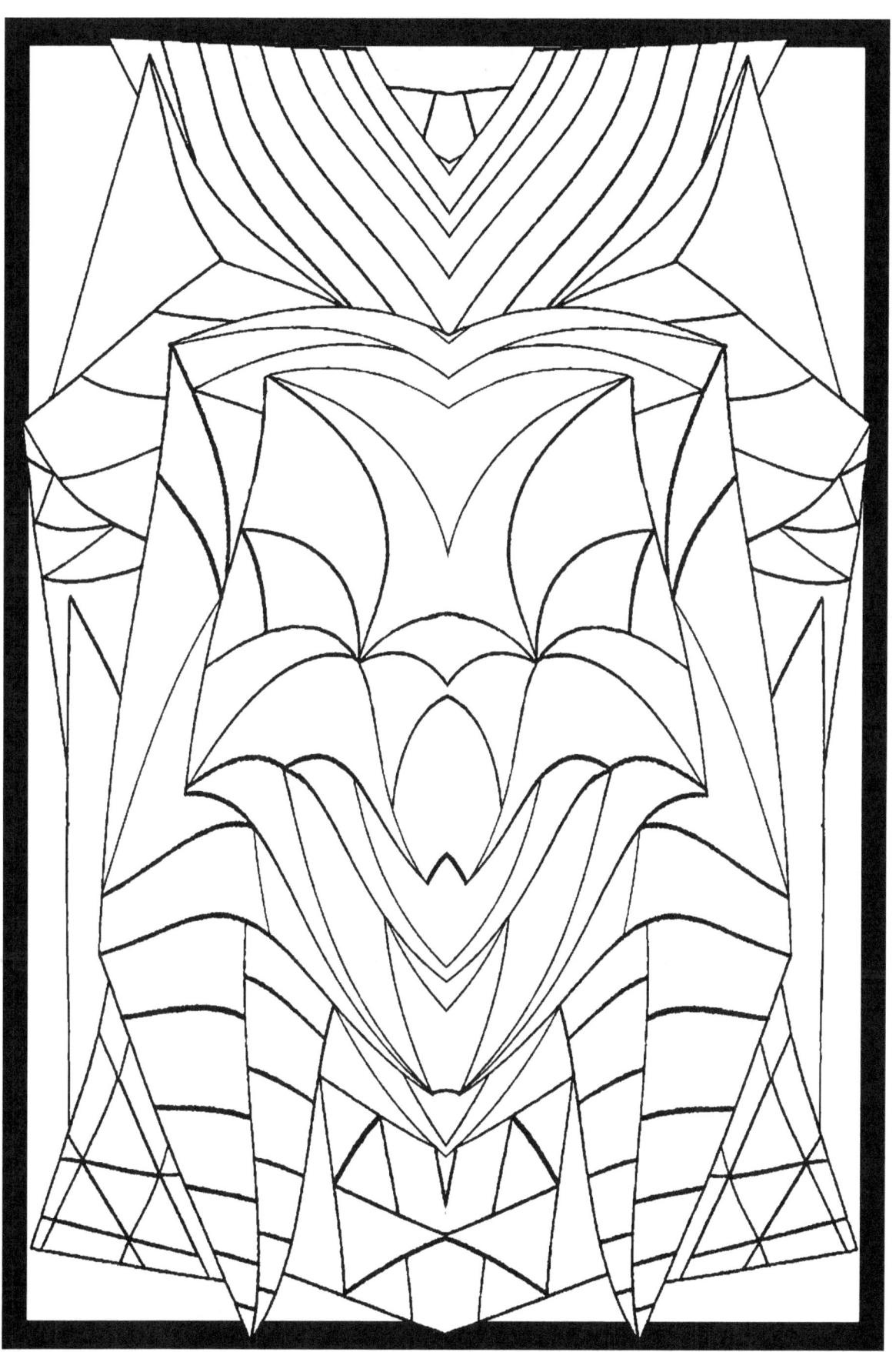

MONSTER REPORT

Monster Name:_____

Originates From:_____

Diet:_____

Description:_____

_____

_____

_____

_____

_____

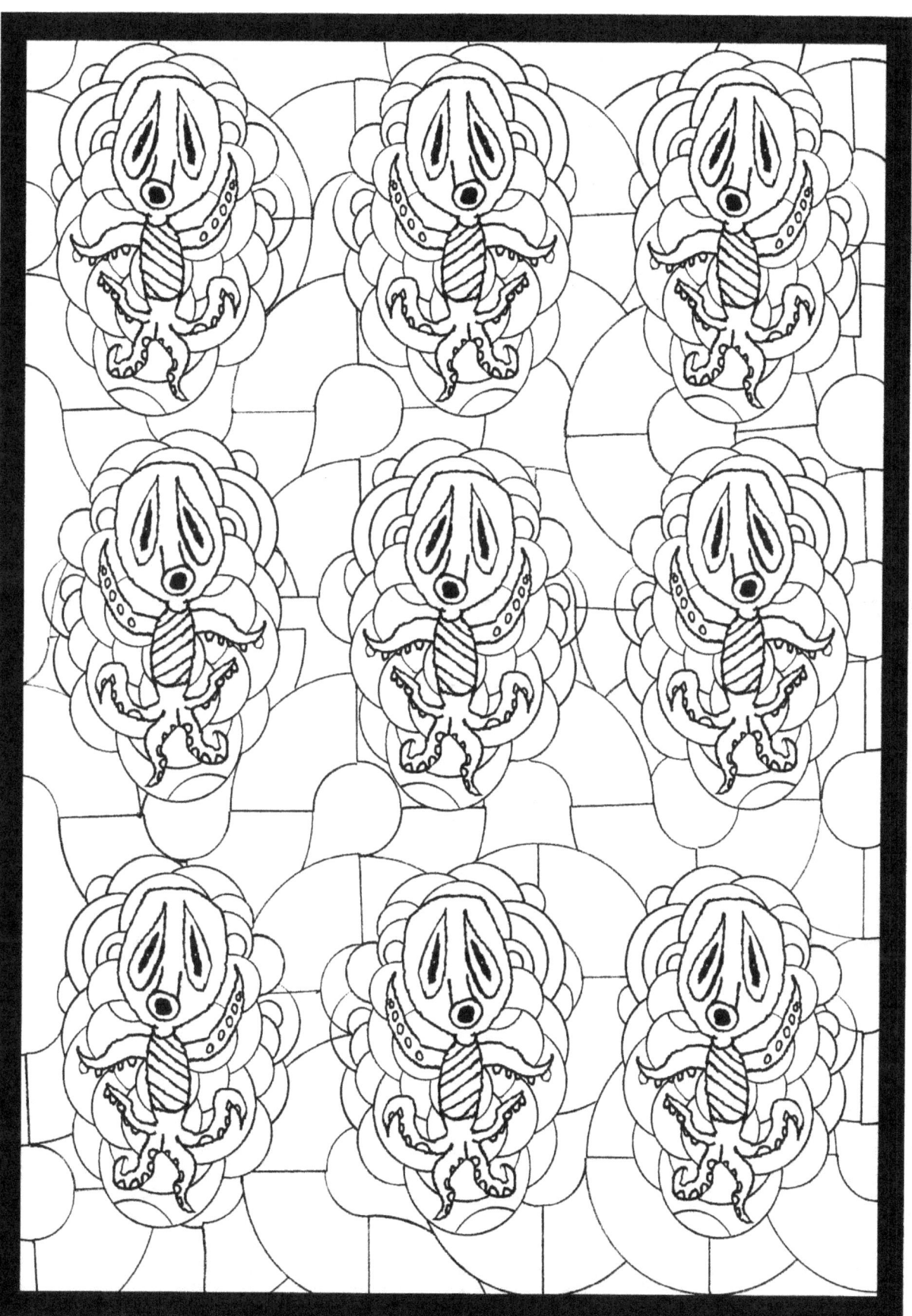

MONSTER REPORT

Monster Name:_____

Originates From:_____

Diet:_____

Description:_____

_____

_____

_____

_____

_____

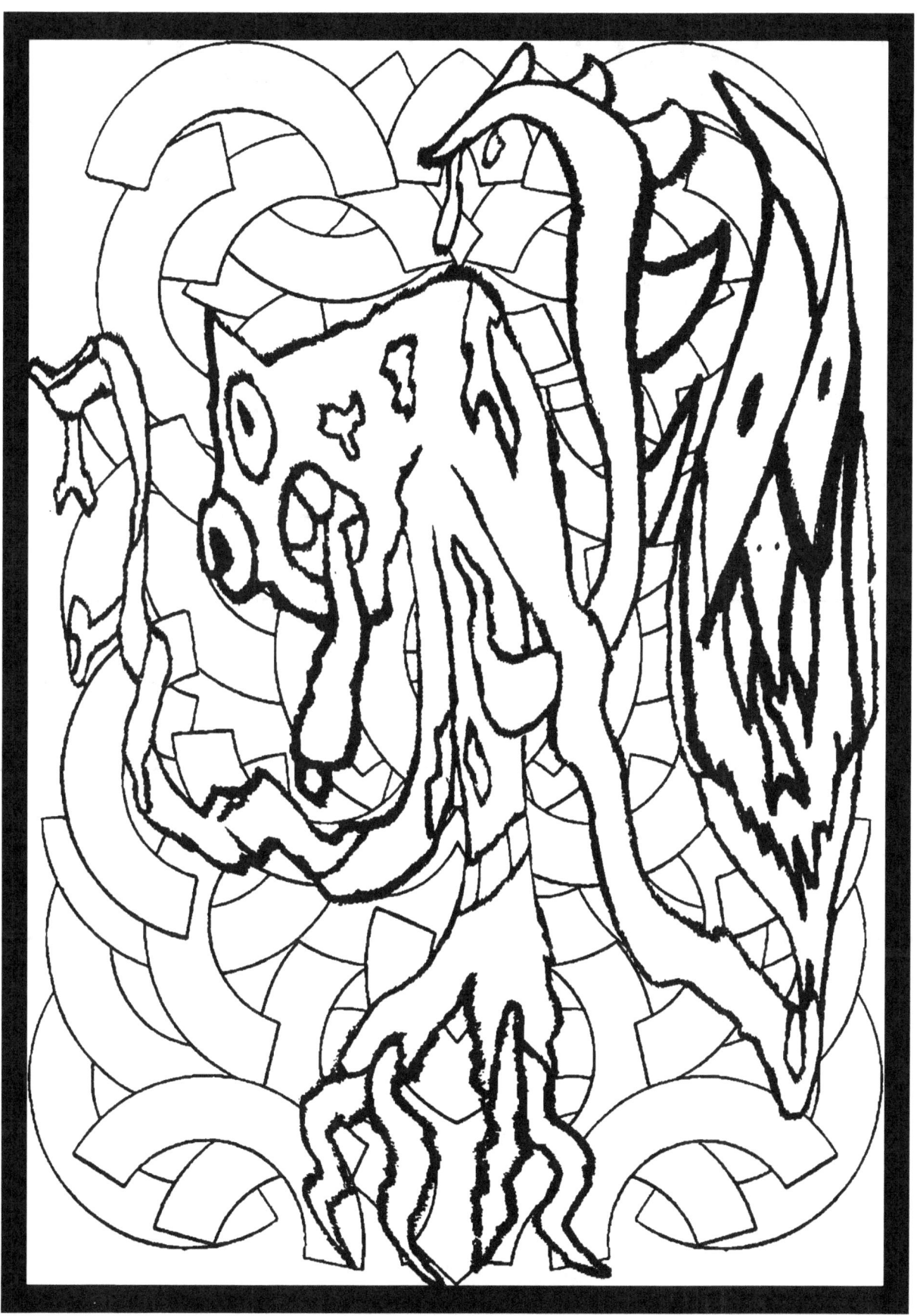

MONSTER REPORT

Monster Name:_____

Originates From:_____

Diet:_____

Description:_____

_____

_____

_____

_____

_____

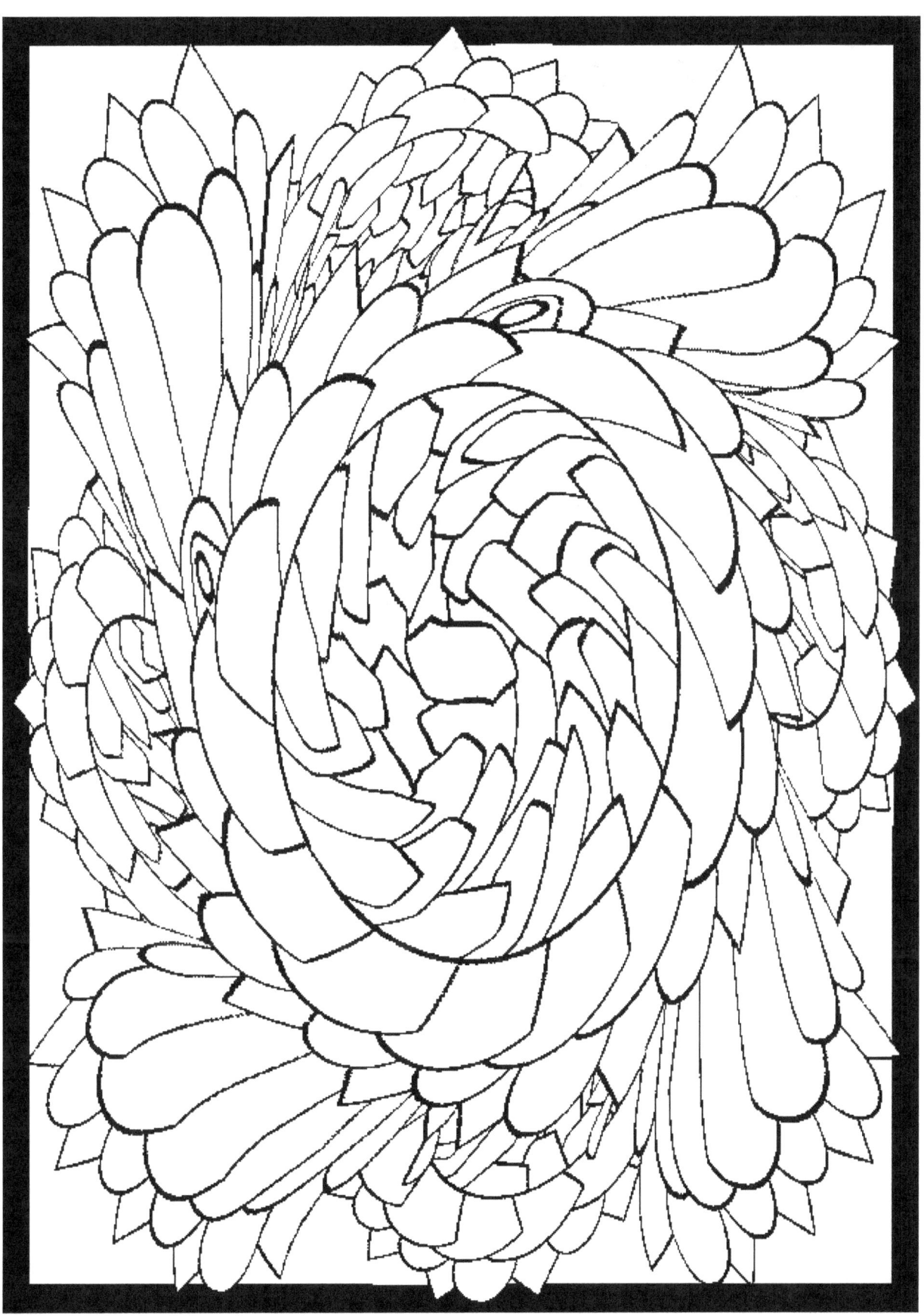

MONSTER REPORT

Monster Name:_____

Originates From:_____

Diet:_____

Description:_____

_____

_____

_____

_____

_____

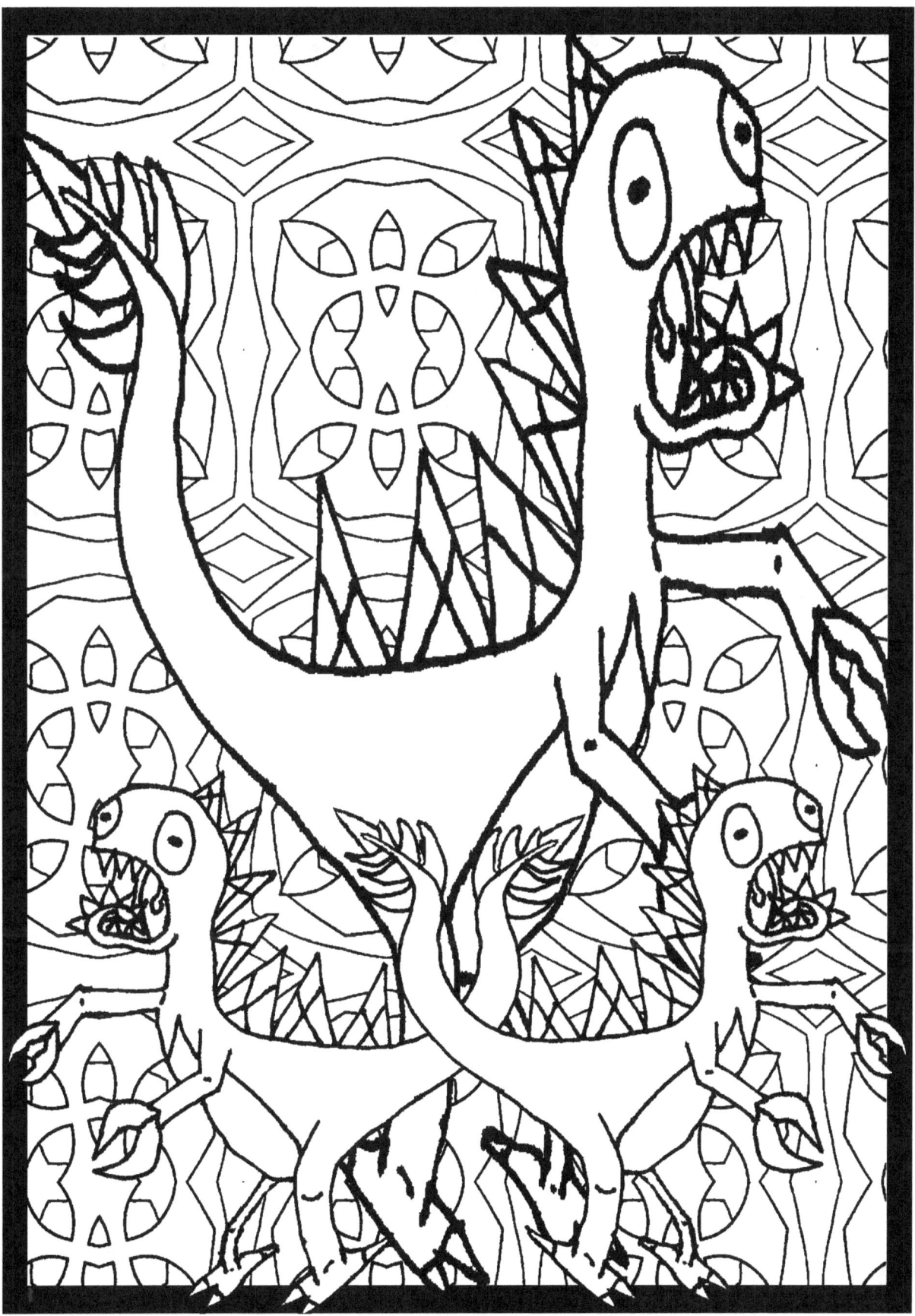

MONSTER REPORT

Monster Name:_____

Originates From:_____

Diet:_____

Description:_____

_____

_____

_____

_____

_____

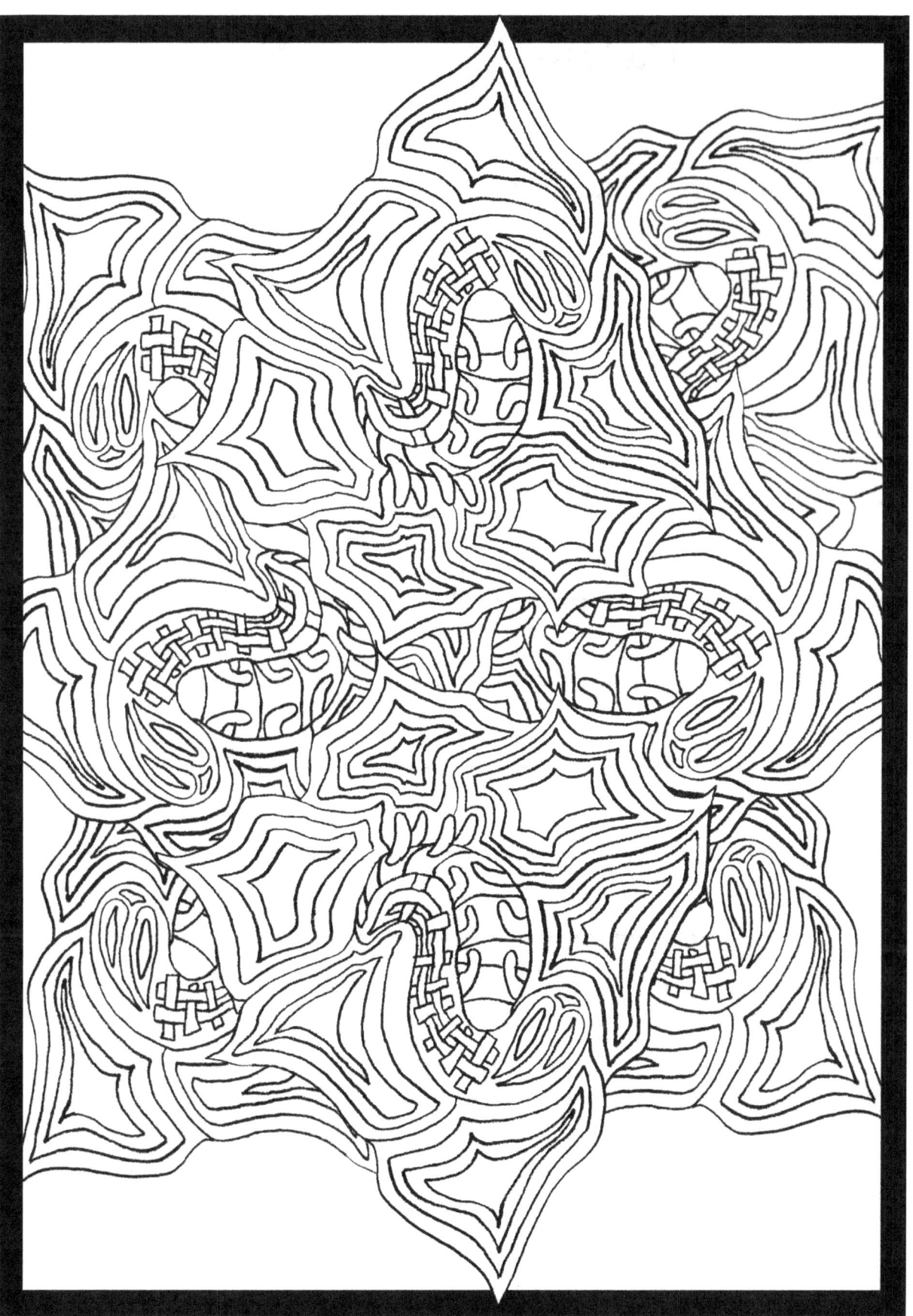

MONSTER REPORT

Monster Name:_____

Originates From:_____

Diet:_____

Description:_____

_____

_____

_____

_____

_____

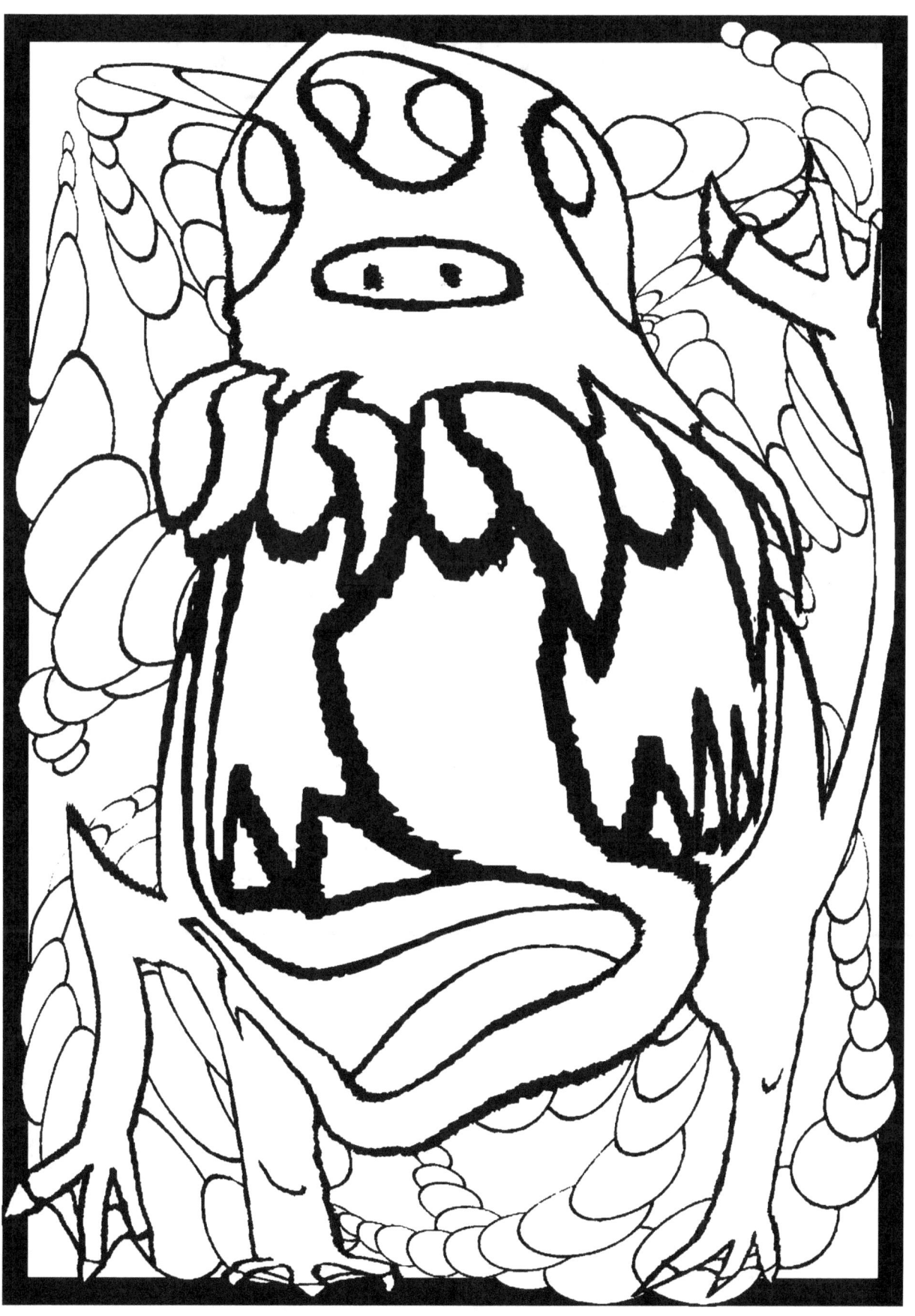

MONSTER REPORT

Monster Name:_____

Originates From:_____

Diet:_____

Description:_____

_____

_____

_____

_____

_____

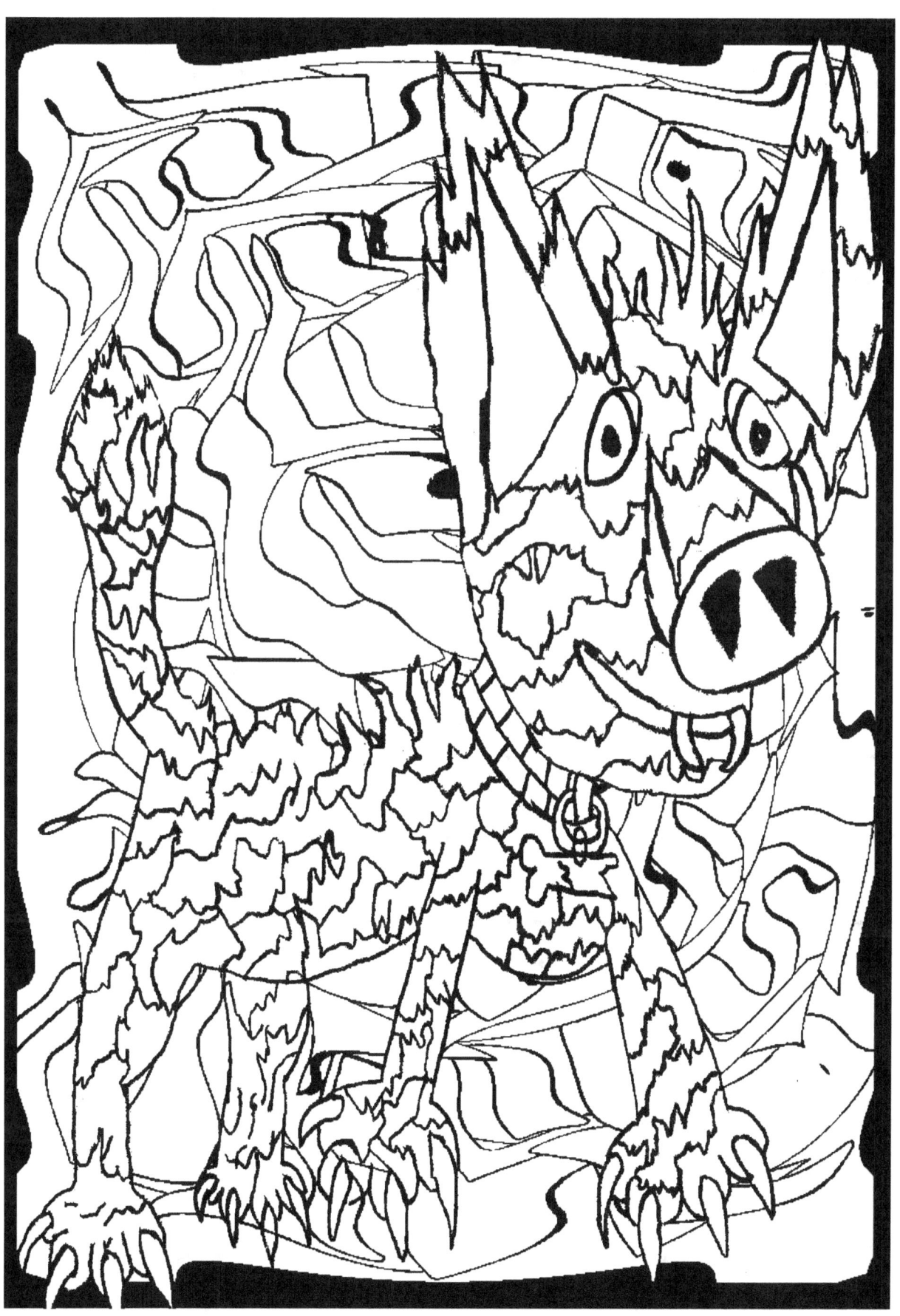

MONSTER REPORT

Monster Name:_____

Originates From:_____

Diet:_____

Description:_____

_____

_____

_____

_____

_____

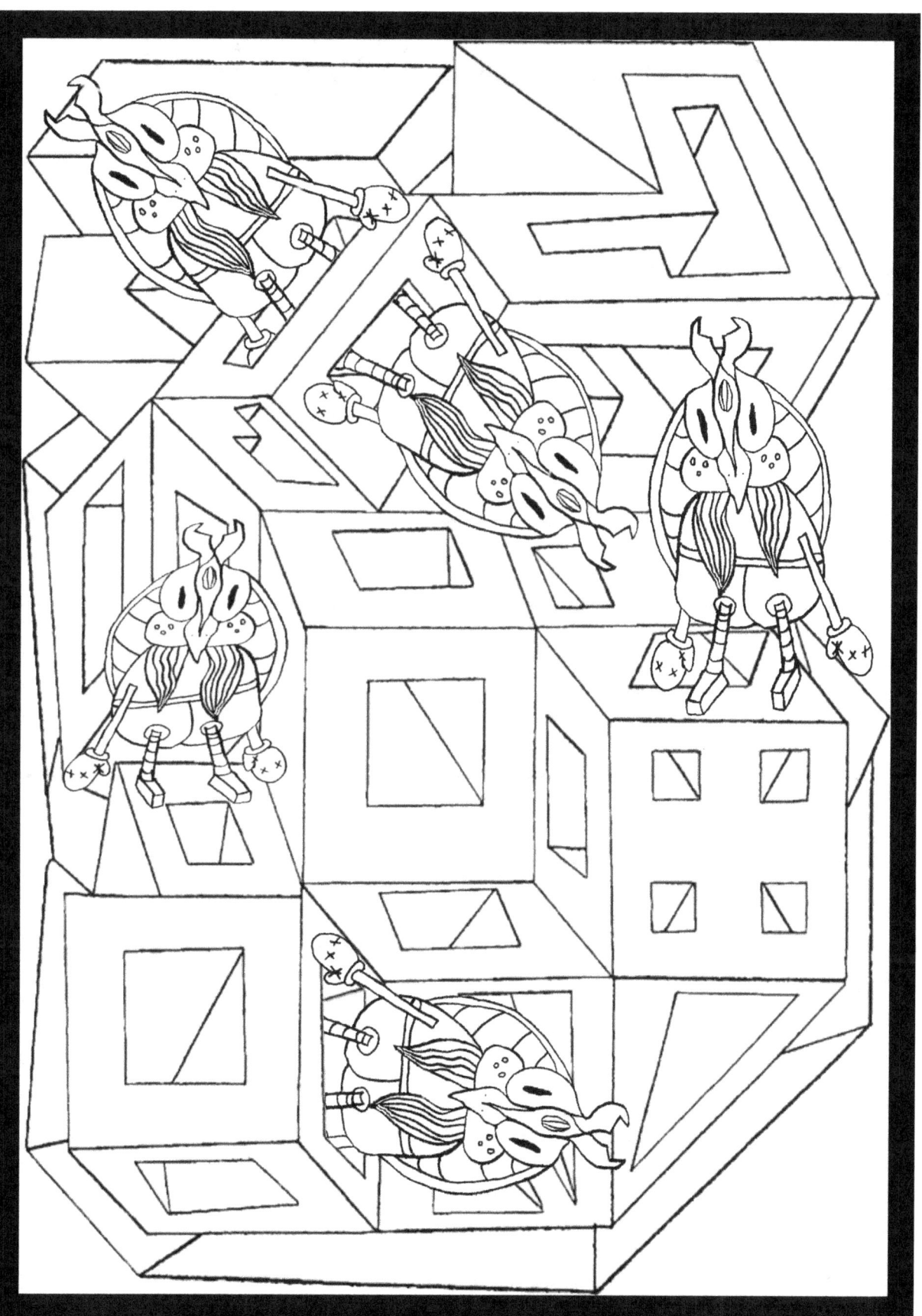

MONSTER REPORT

Monster Name:_____

Originates From:_____

Diet:_____

Description:_____

_____

_____

_____

_____

_____

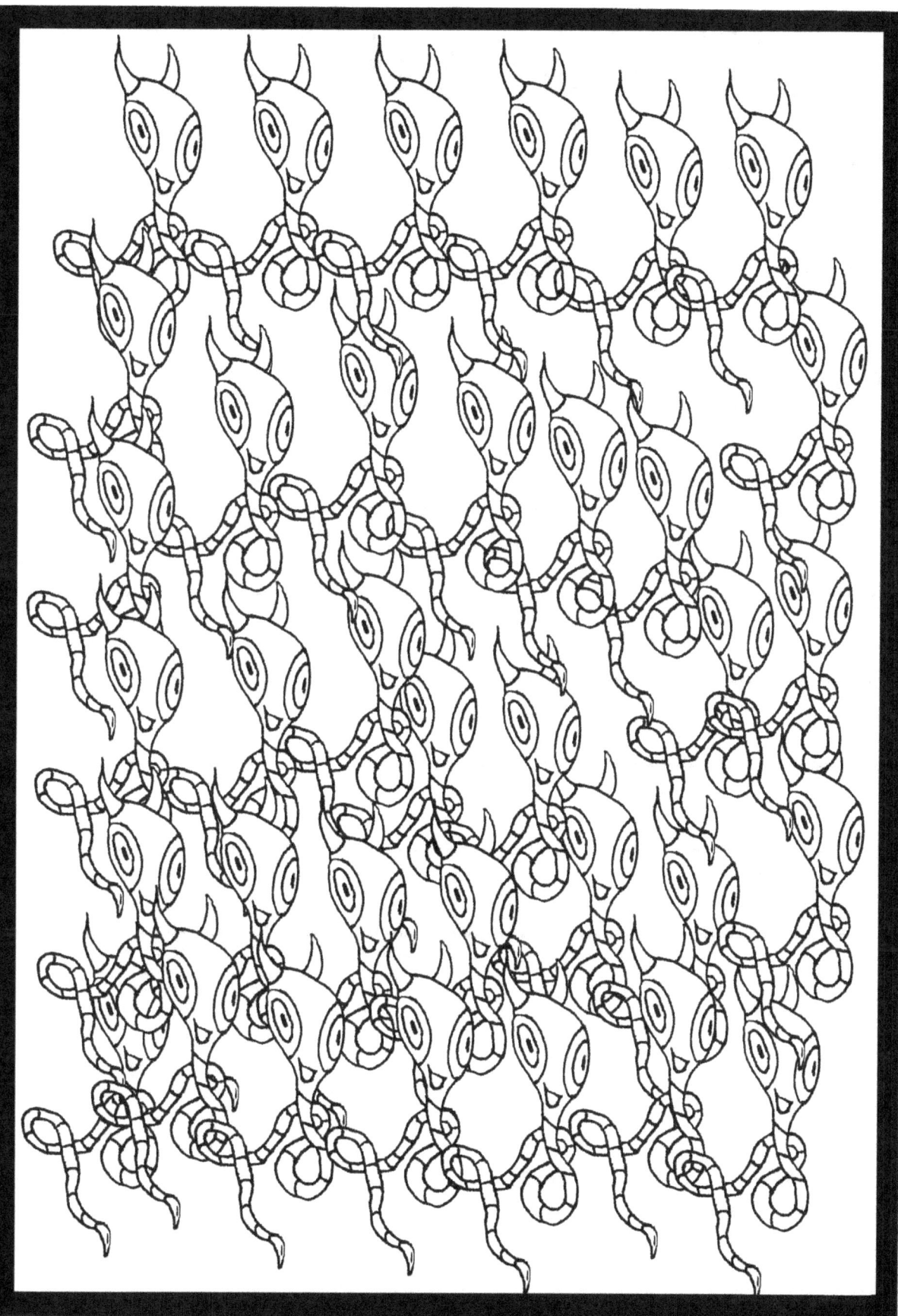

MONSTER REPORT

Monster Name:_____

Originates From:_____

Diet:_____

Description:_____

_____

_____

_____

_____

_____

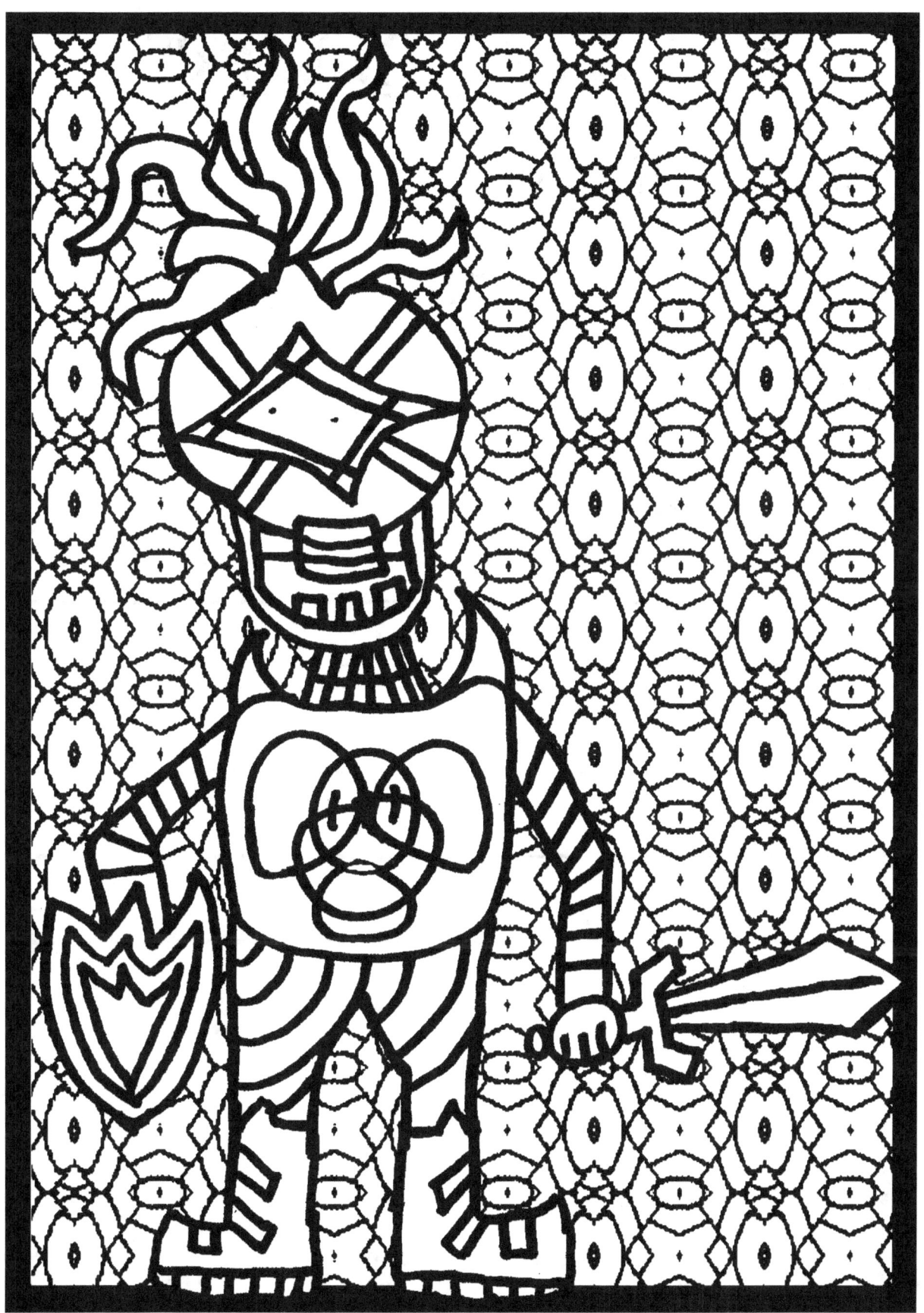

MONSTER REPORT

Monster Name:_____

Originates From:_____

Diet:_____

Description:_____

_____

_____

_____

_____

_____

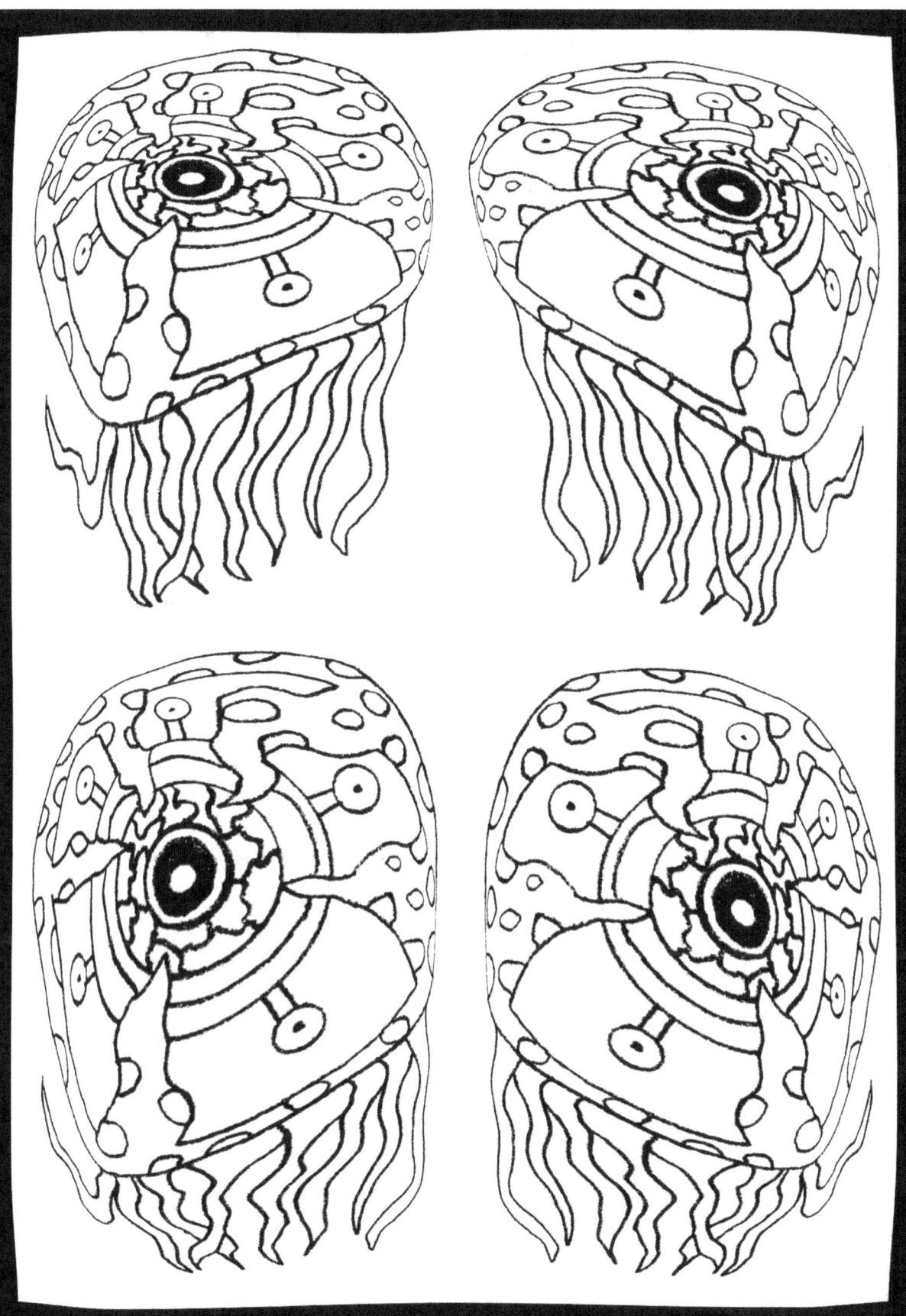

MONSTER REPORT

Monster Name:_____

Originates From:_____

Diet:_____

Description:_____

_____

_____

_____

_____

_____

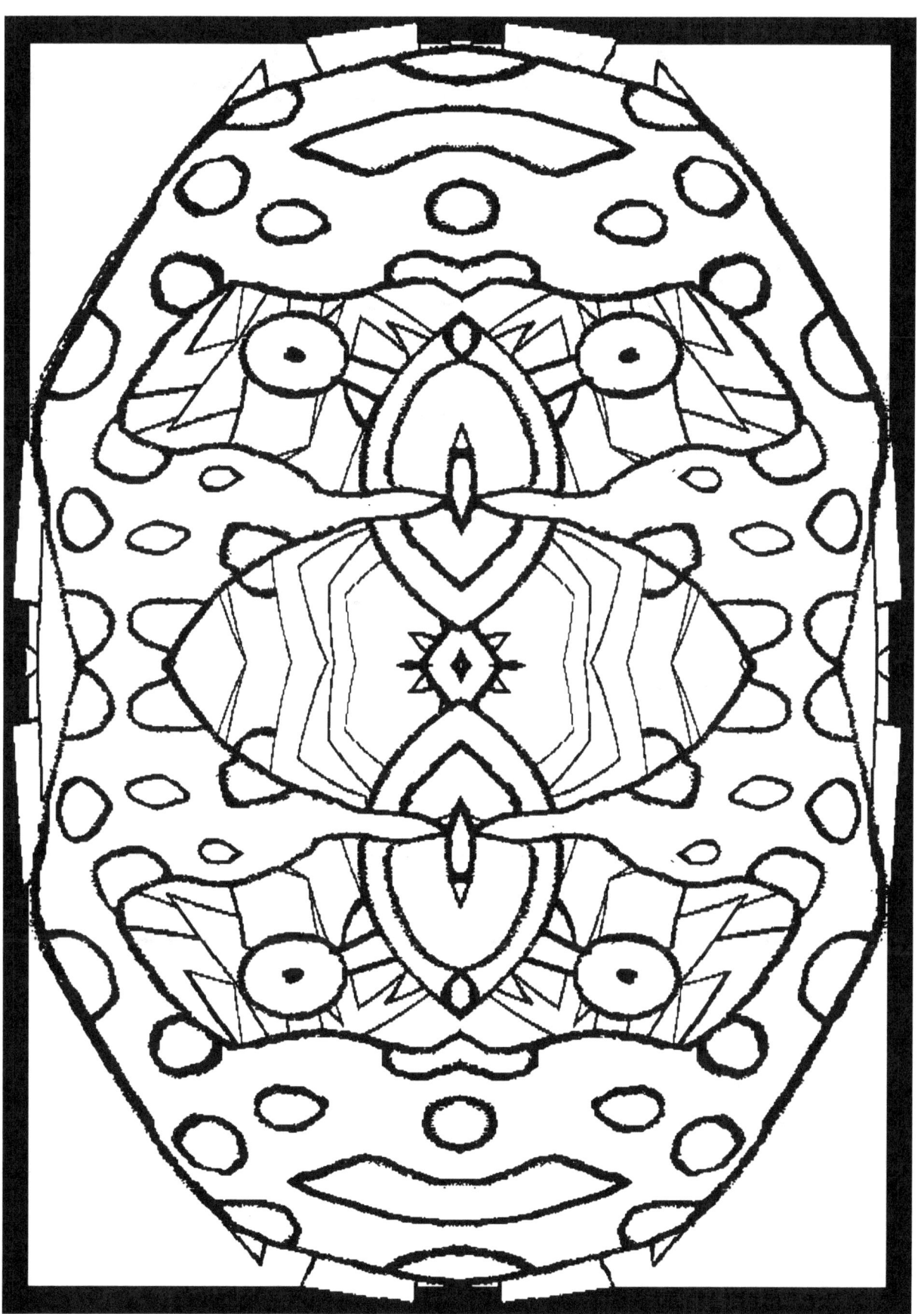

MONSTER REPORT

Monster Name:_____

Originates From:_____

Diet:_____

Description:_____

_____

_____

_____

_____

_____

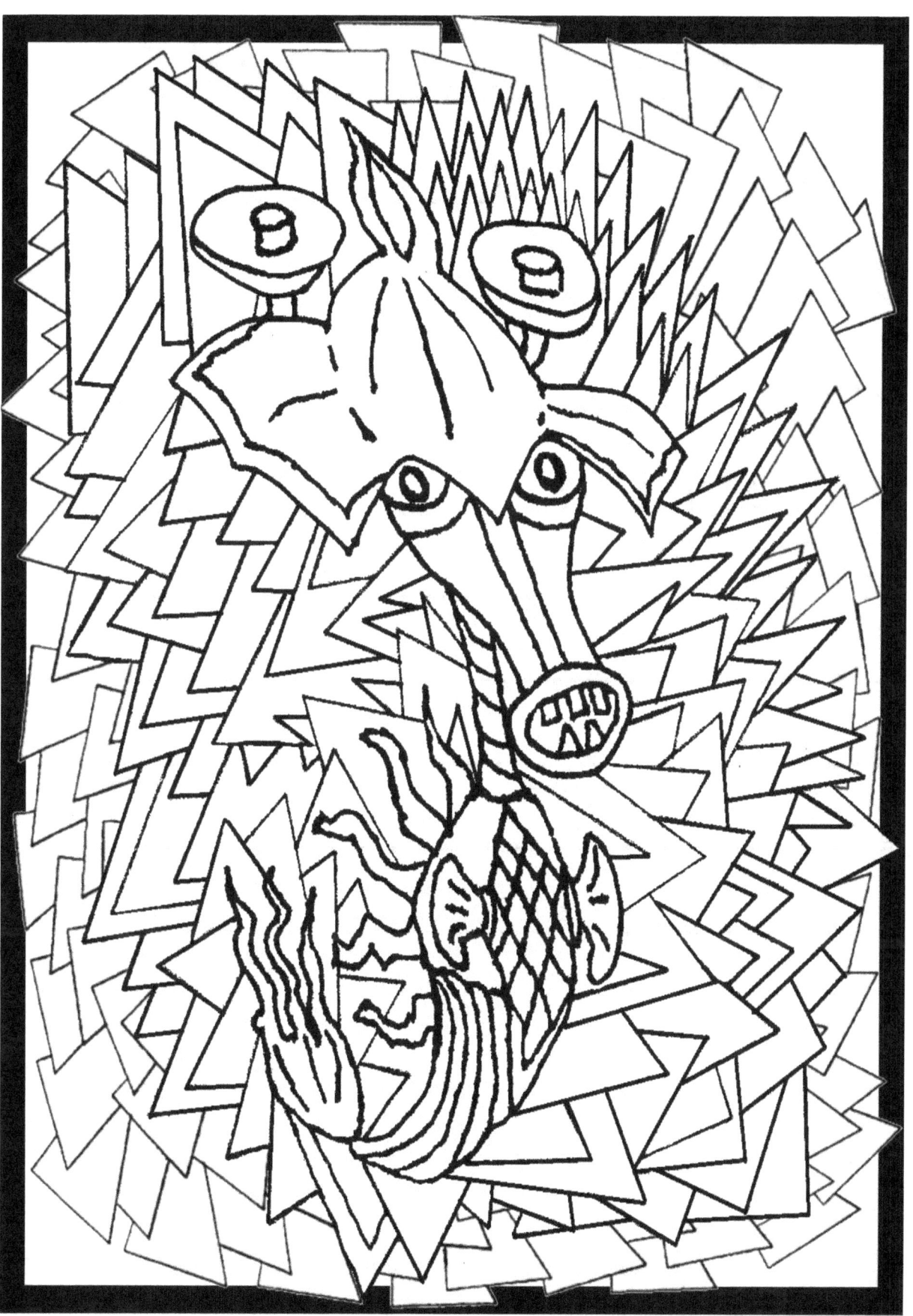

MONSTER REPORT

Monster Name:_____

Originates From:_____

Diet:_____

Description:_____

_____

_____

_____

_____

_____

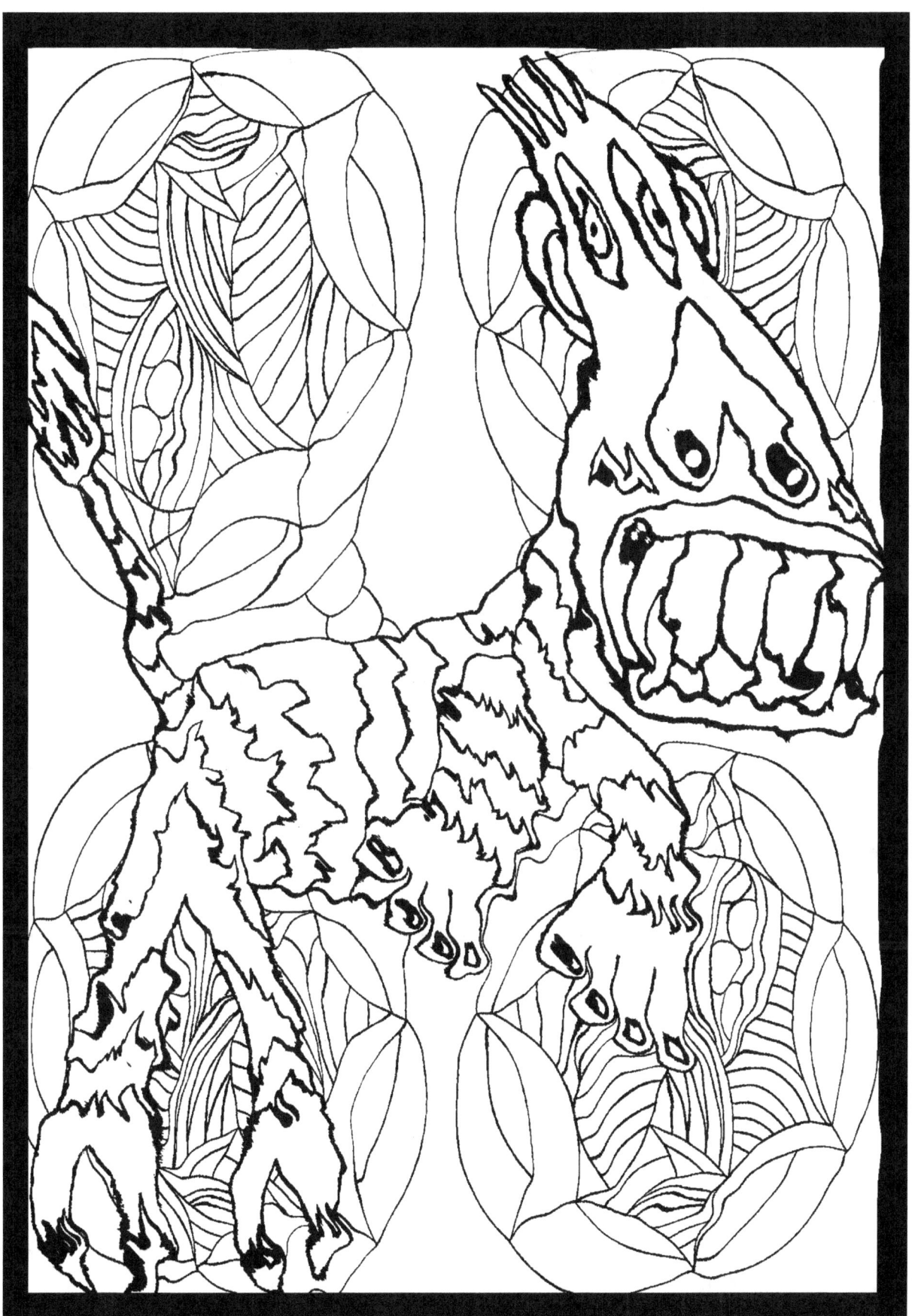

MONSTER REPORT

Monster Name:_____

Originates From:_____

Diet:_____

Description:_____

_____

_____

_____

_____

_____

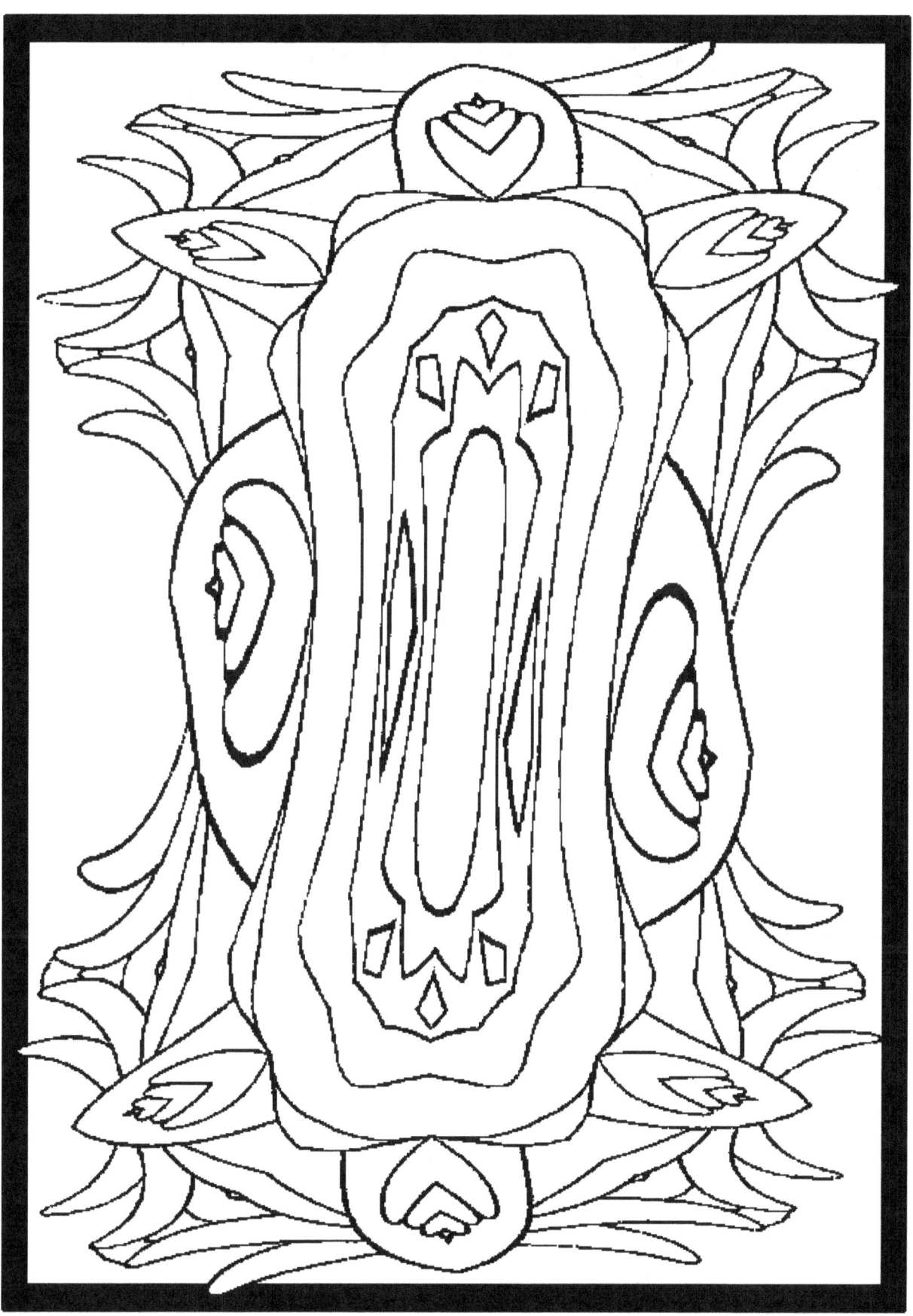

MONSTER REPORT

Monster Name:_____

Originates From:_____

Diet:_____

Description:_____

_____

_____

_____

_____

_____

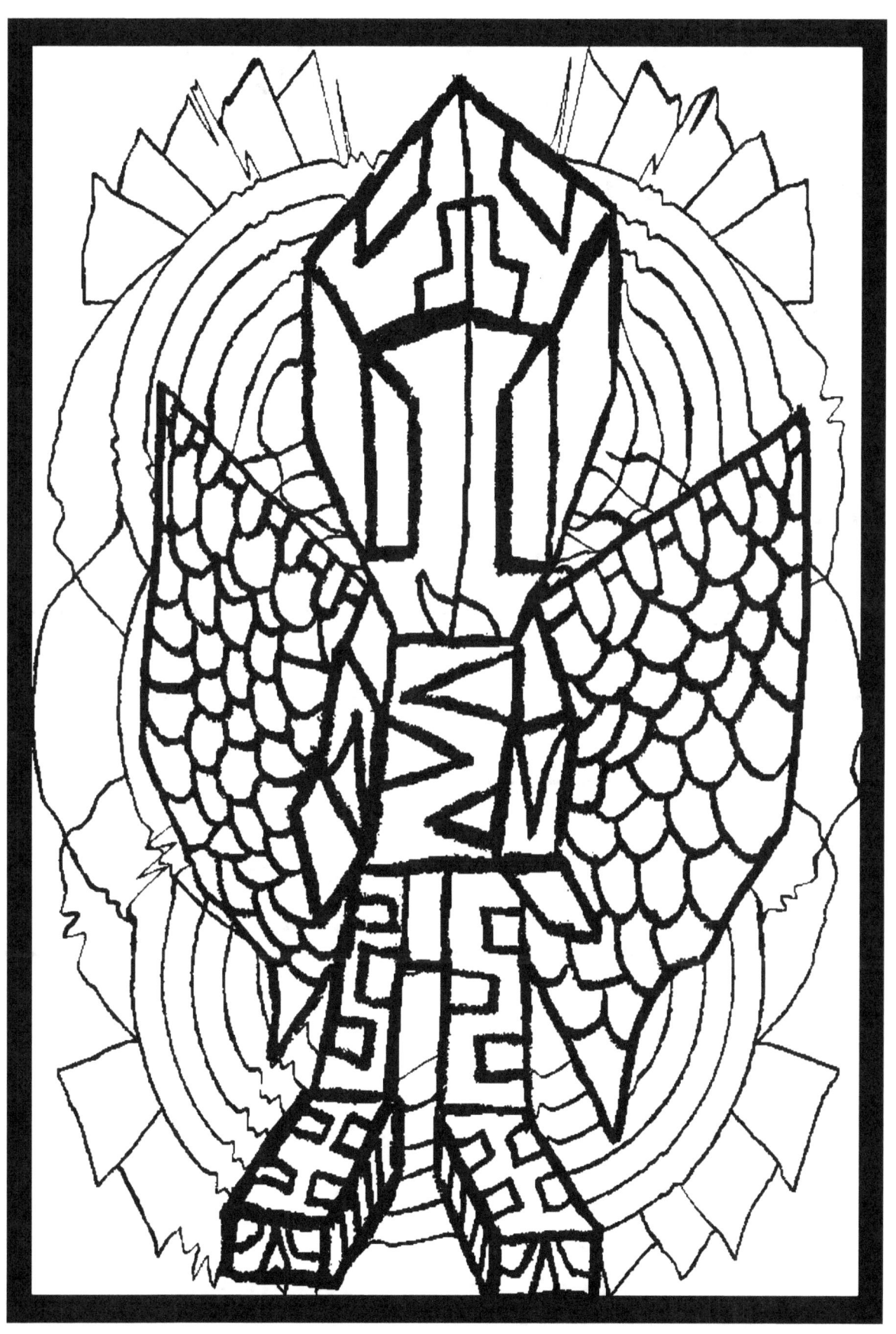

MONSTER REPORT

Monster Name:_____

Originates From:_____

Diet:_____

Description:_____

_____

_____

_____

_____

_____

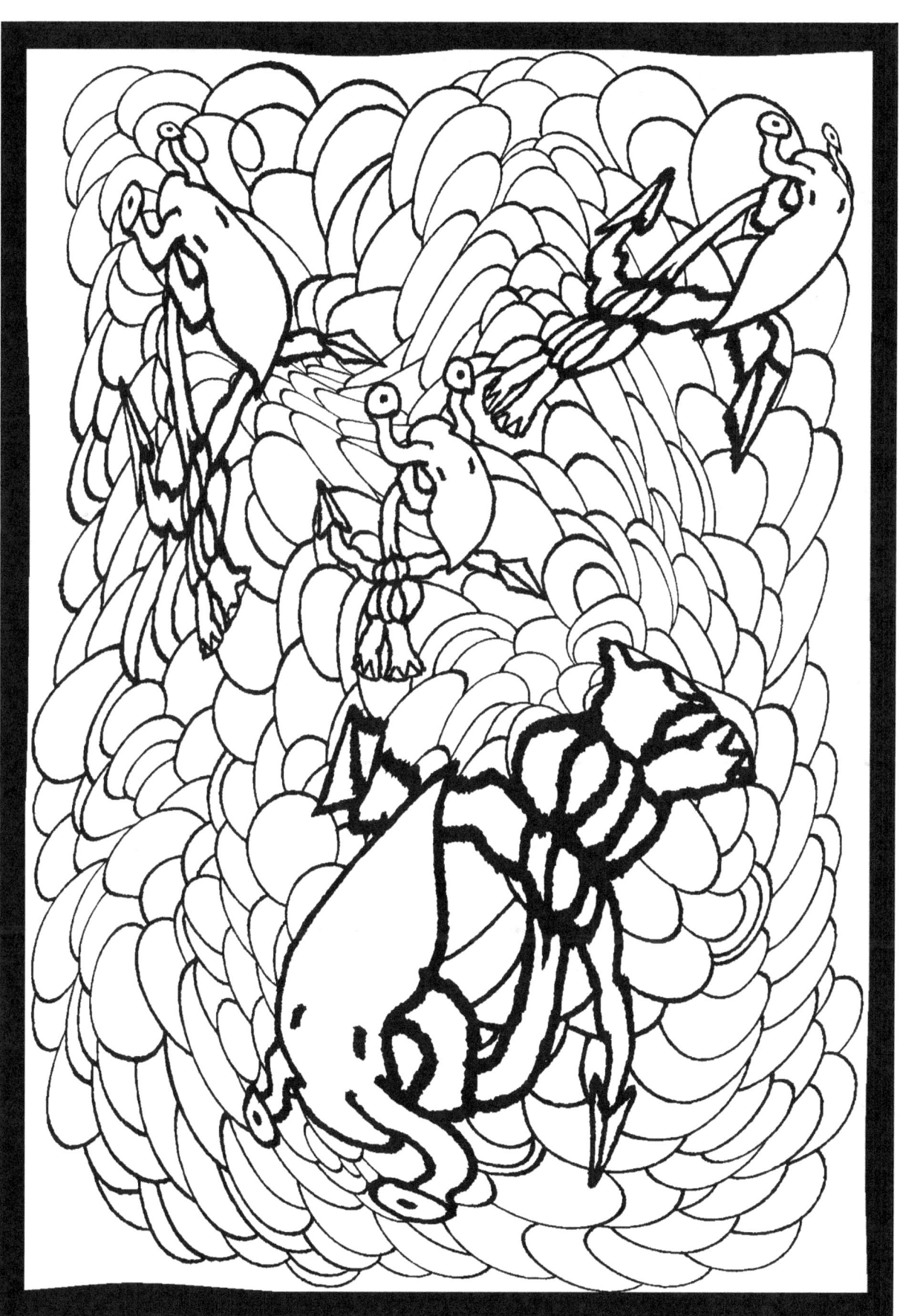

MONSTER REPORT

Monster Name:_____

Originates From:_____

Diet:_____

Description:_____

_____

_____

_____

_____

_____

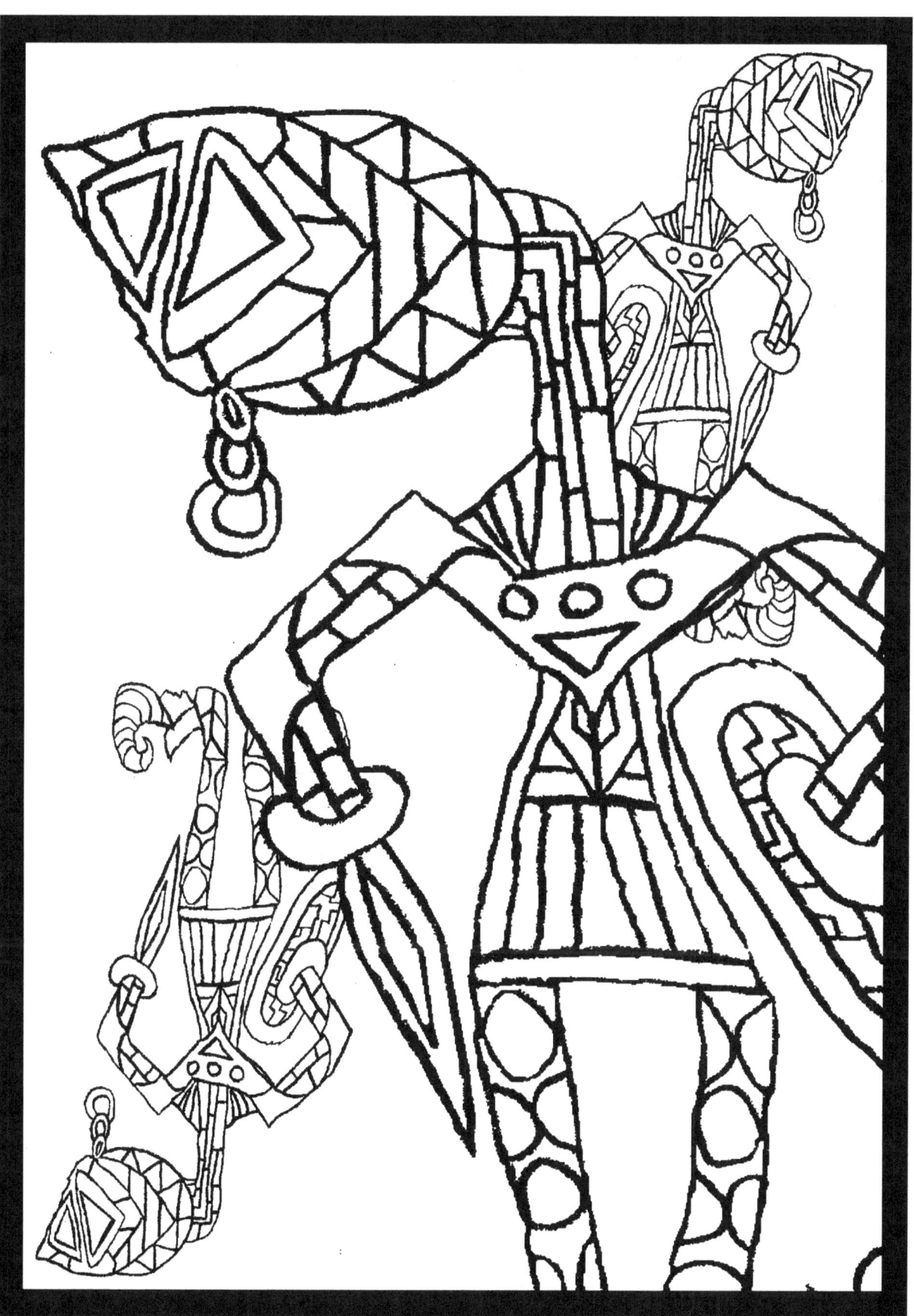

MONSTER REPORT

Monster Name:_____

Originates From:_____

Diet:_____

Description:_____

_____

_____

_____

_____

_____

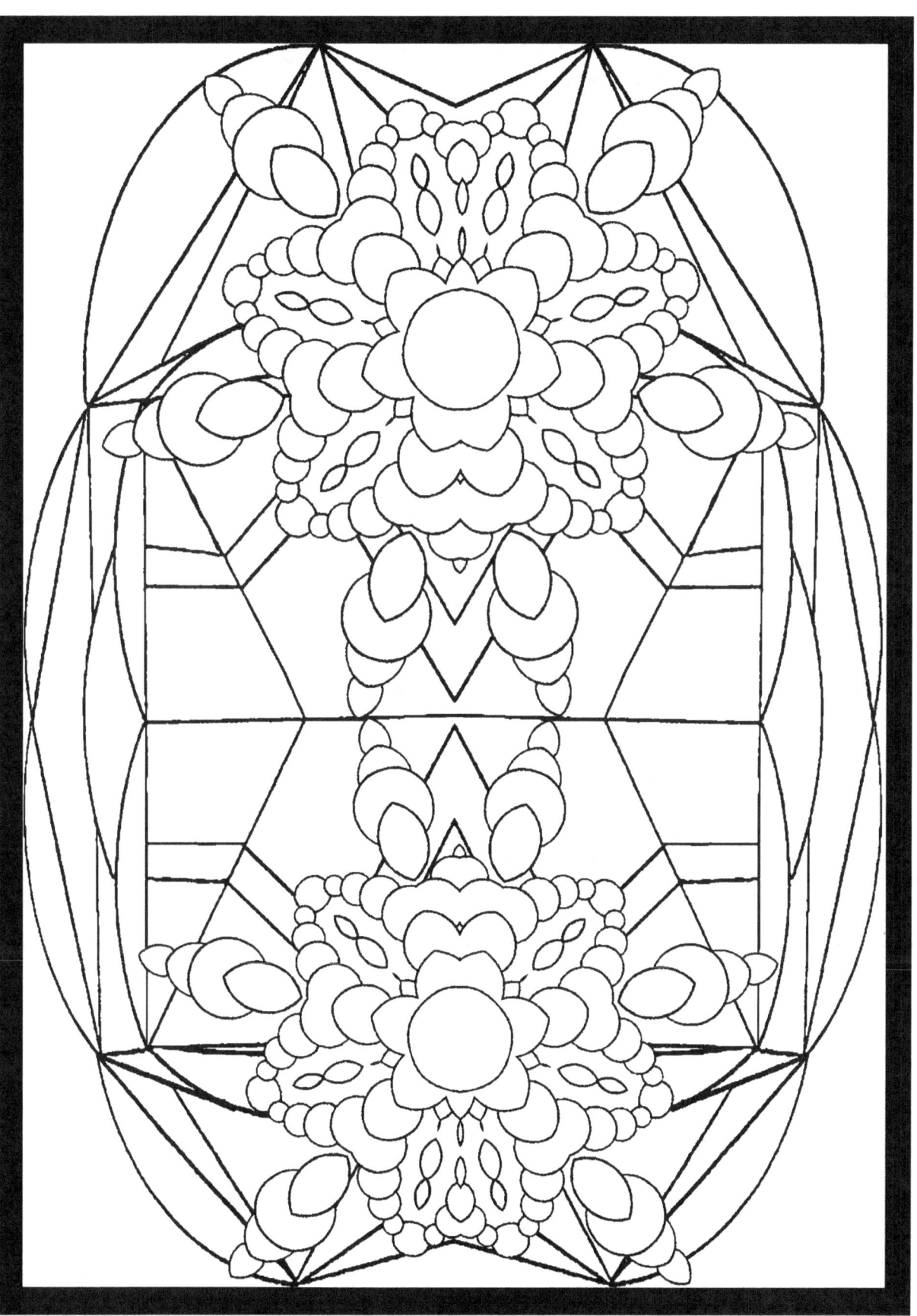

MONSTER REPORT

Monster Name:_____

Originates From:_____

Diet:_____

Description:_____

_____

_____

_____

_____

_____

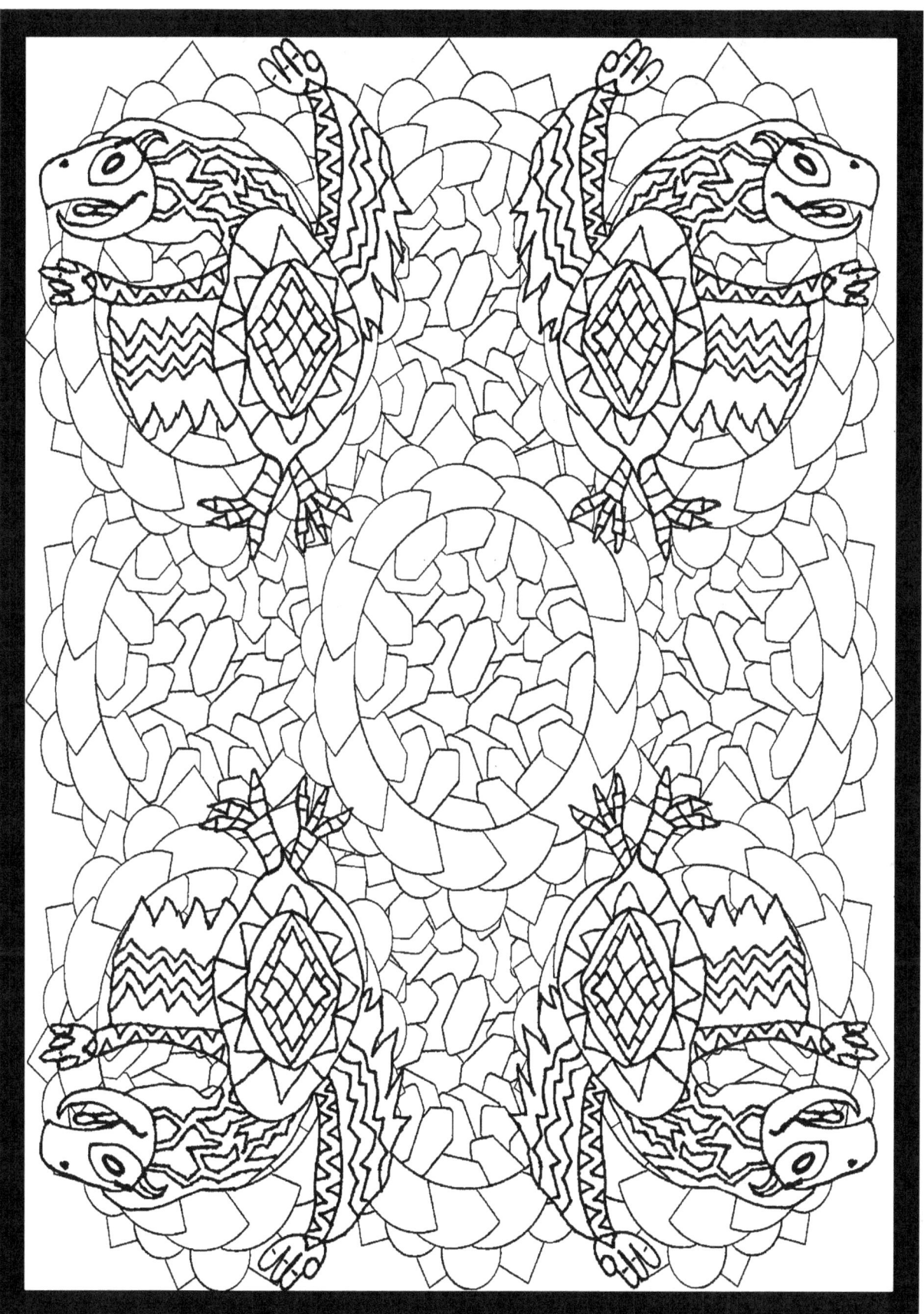

MONSTER REPORT

Monster Name:_____

Originates From:_____

Diet:_____

Description:_____

_____

_____

_____

_____

_____

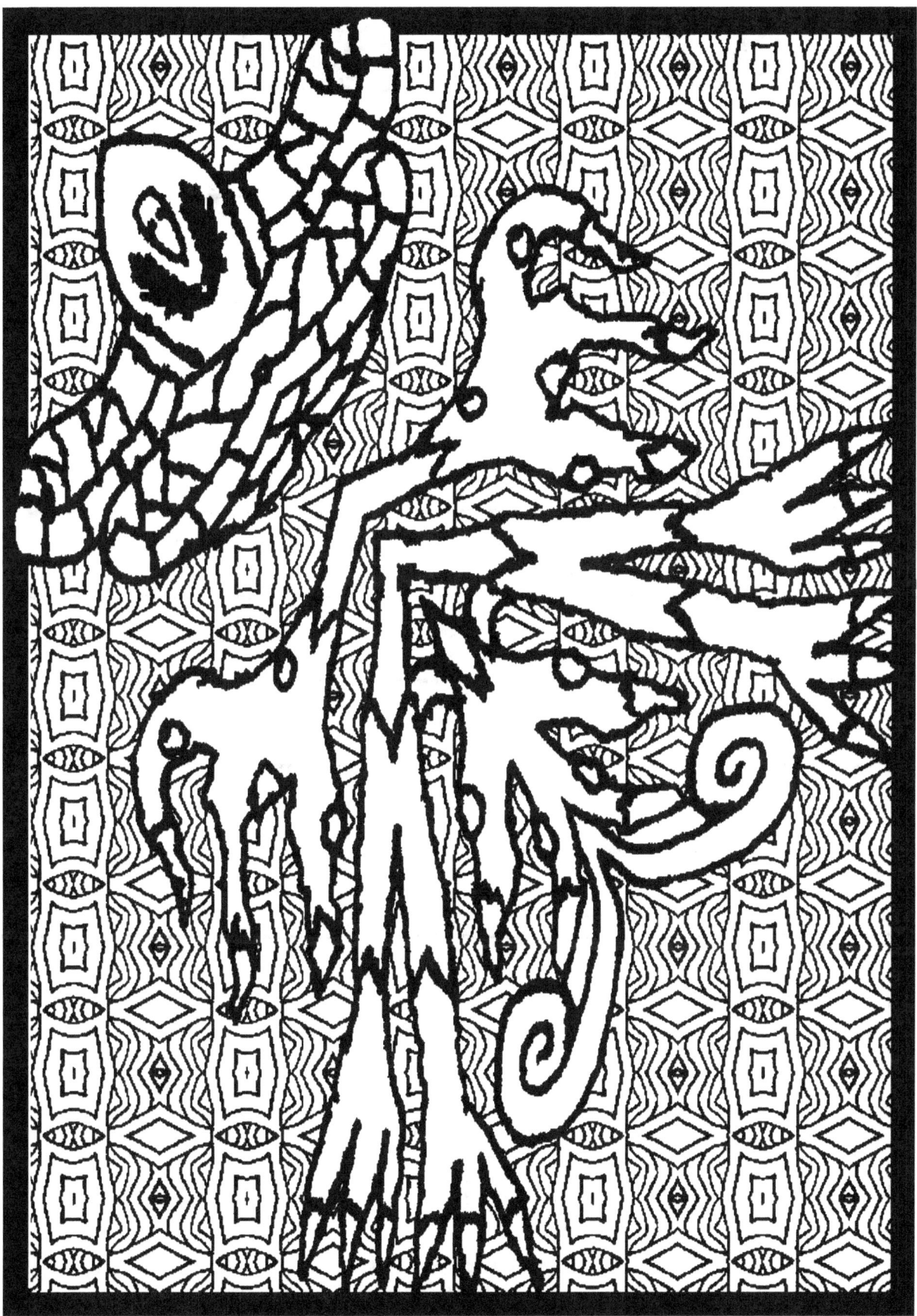

MONSTER REPORT

Monster Name:_____

Originates From:_____

Diet:_____

Description:_____

_____

_____

_____

_____

_____

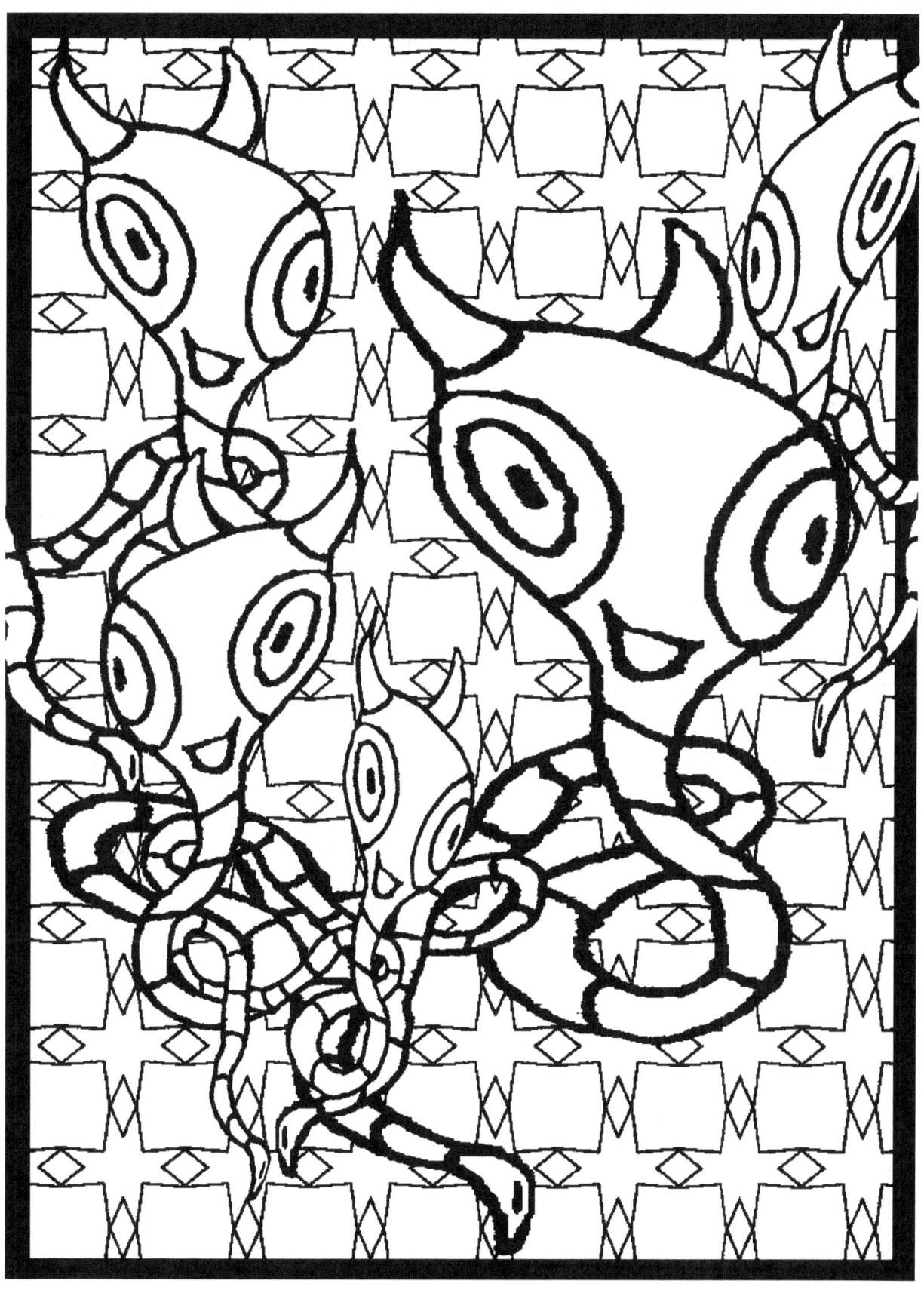

MONSTER REPORT

Monster Name:_____

Originates From:_____

Diet:_____

Description:_____

_____

_____

_____

_____

_____

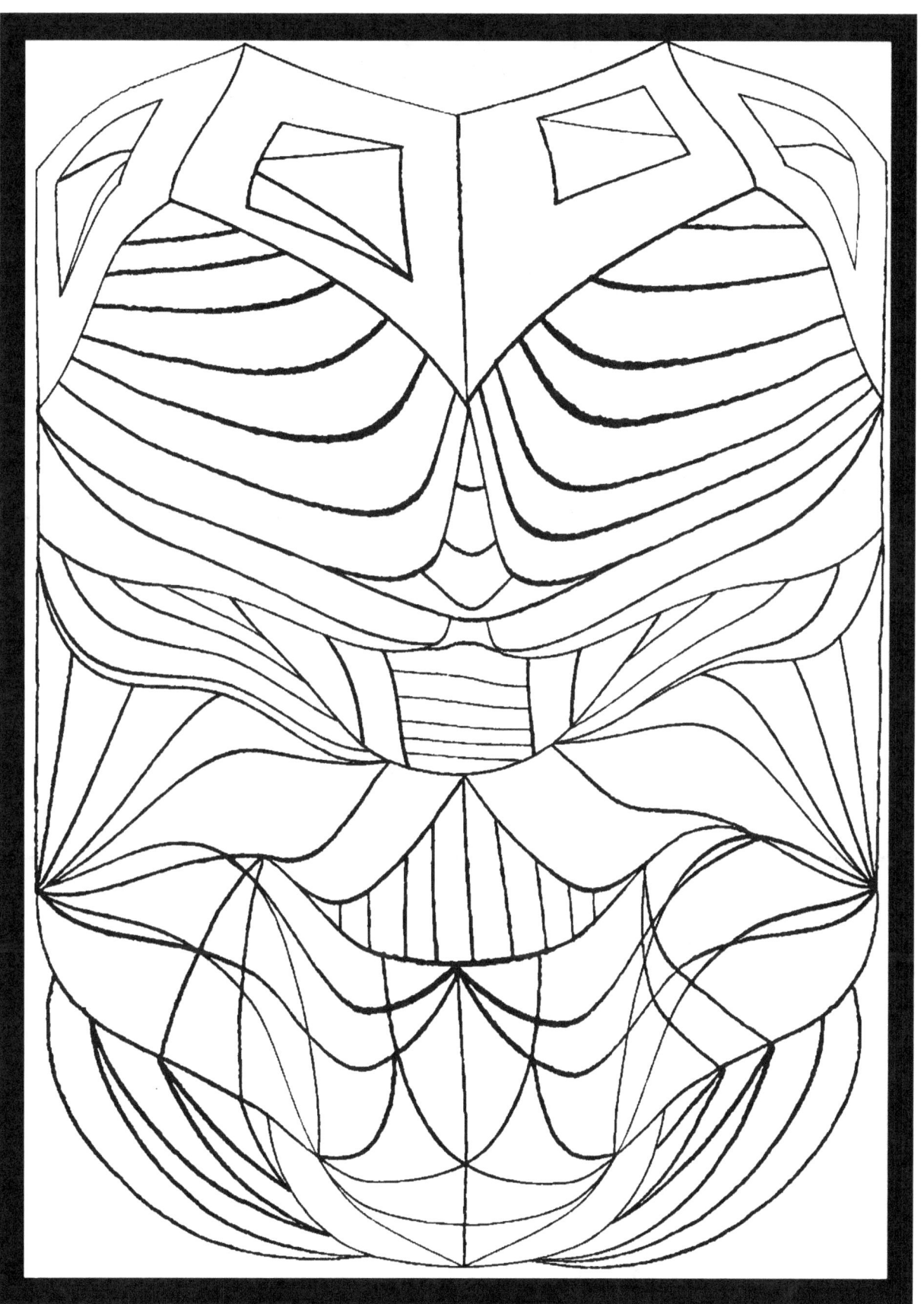

MONSTER REPORT

Monster Name:_____

Originates From:_____

Diet:_____

Description:_____

_____

_____

_____

_____

_____

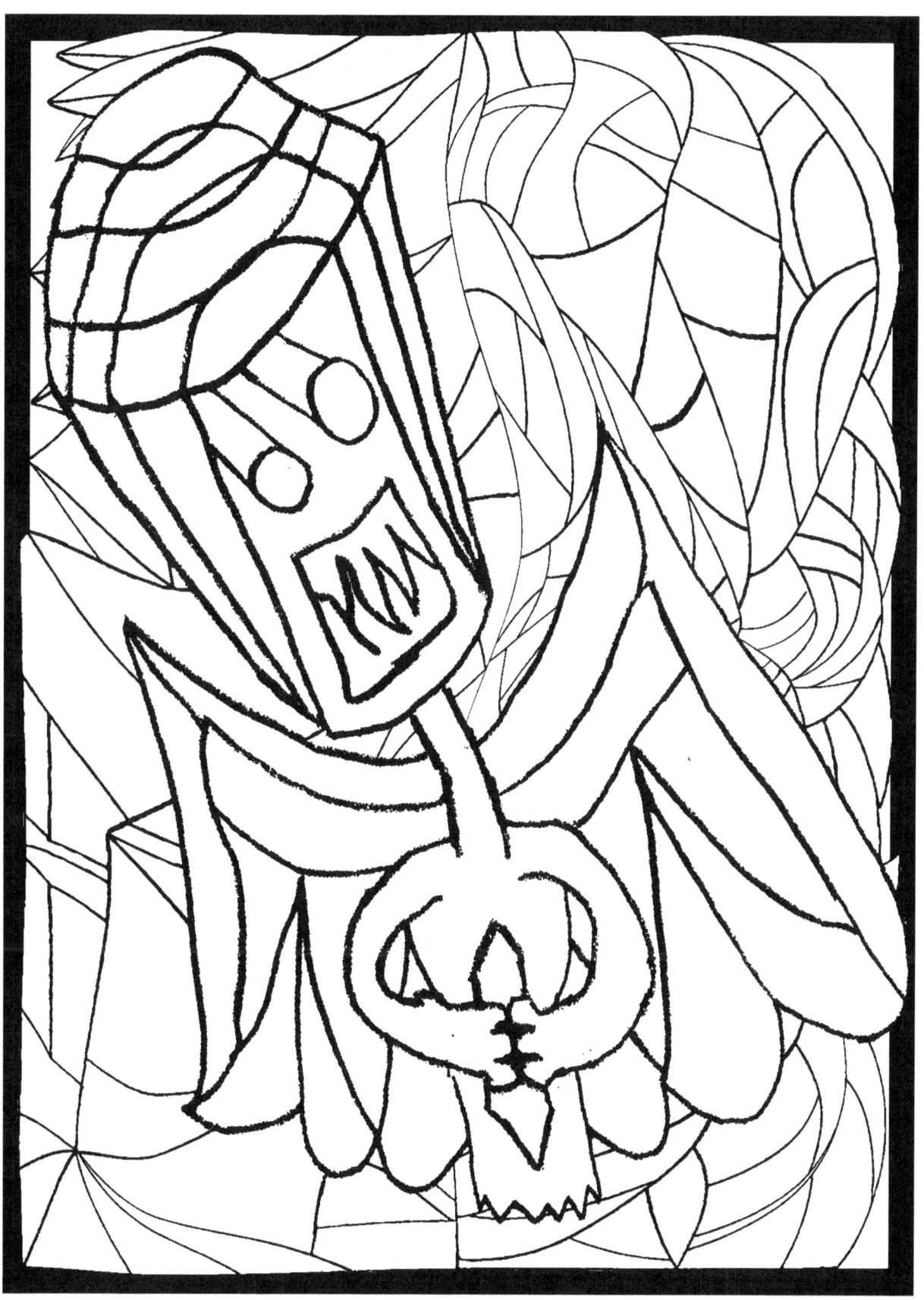

MONSTER REPORT

Monster Name:_____

Originates From:_____

Diet:_____

Description:_____

_____

_____

_____

_____

_____

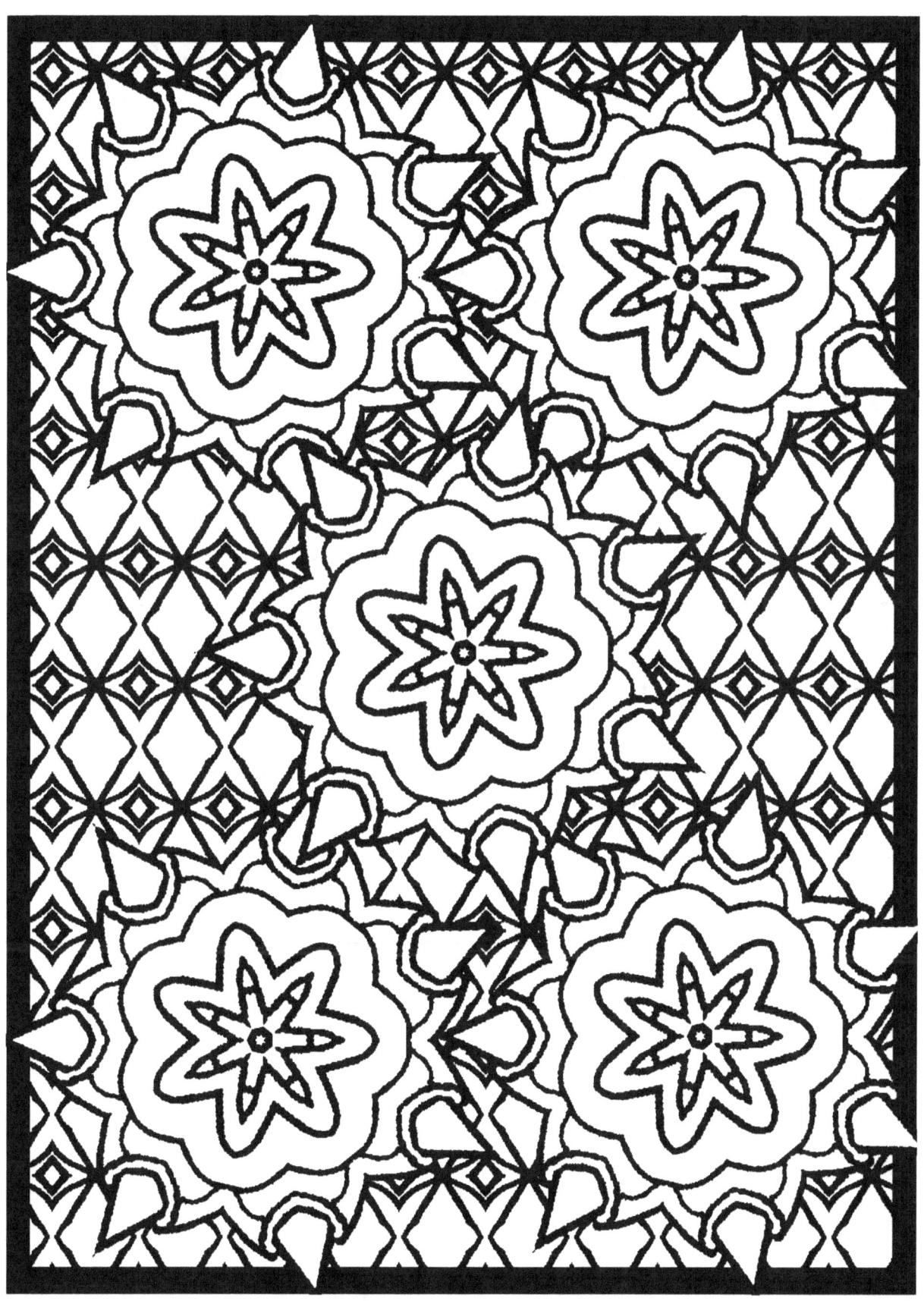

MONSTER REPORT

Monster Name:_____

Originates From:_____

Diet:_____

Description:_____

_____

_____

_____

_____

_____

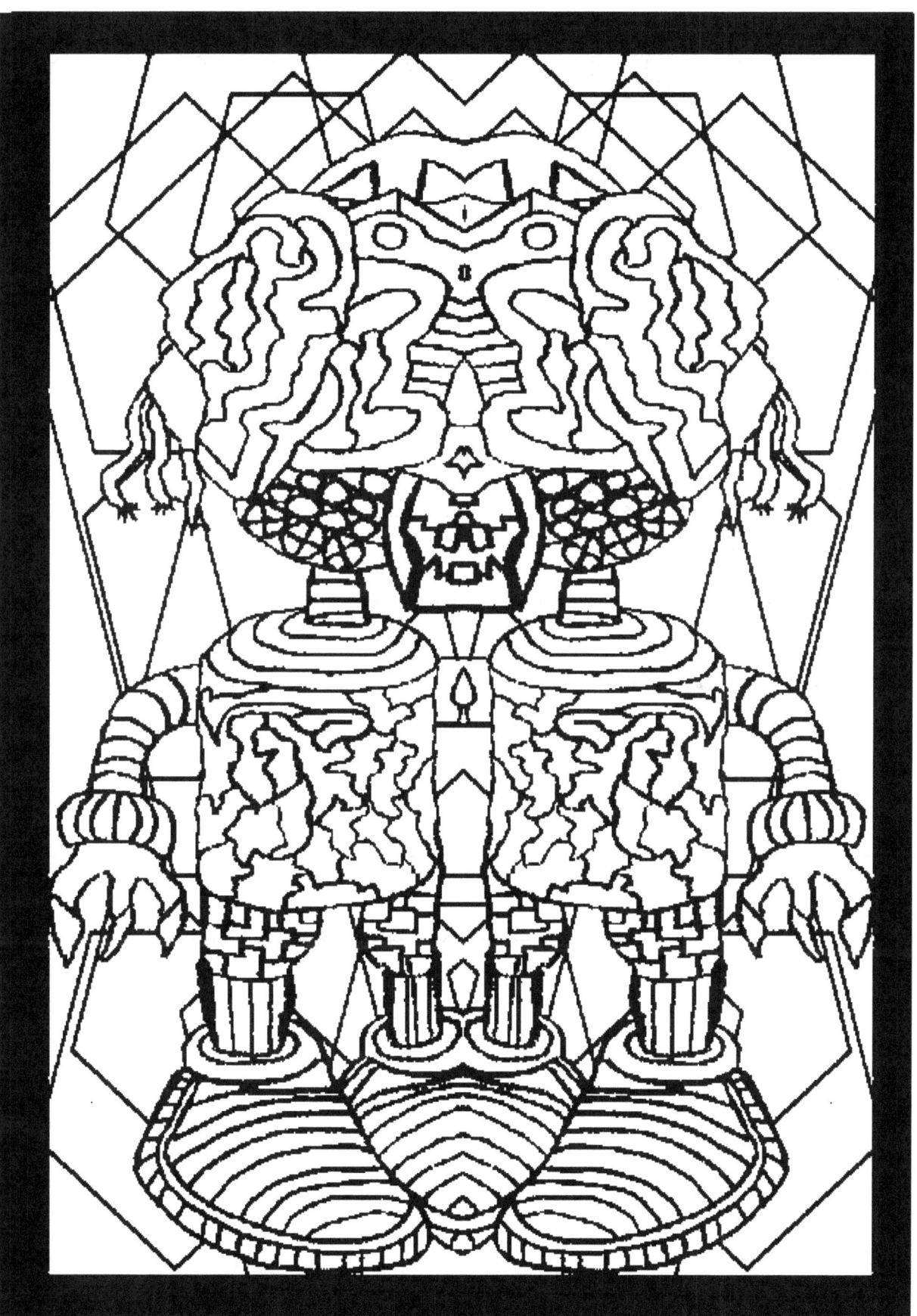

MONSTER REPORT

Monster Name:_____

Originates From:_____

Diet:_____

Description:_____

_____

_____

_____

_____

_____

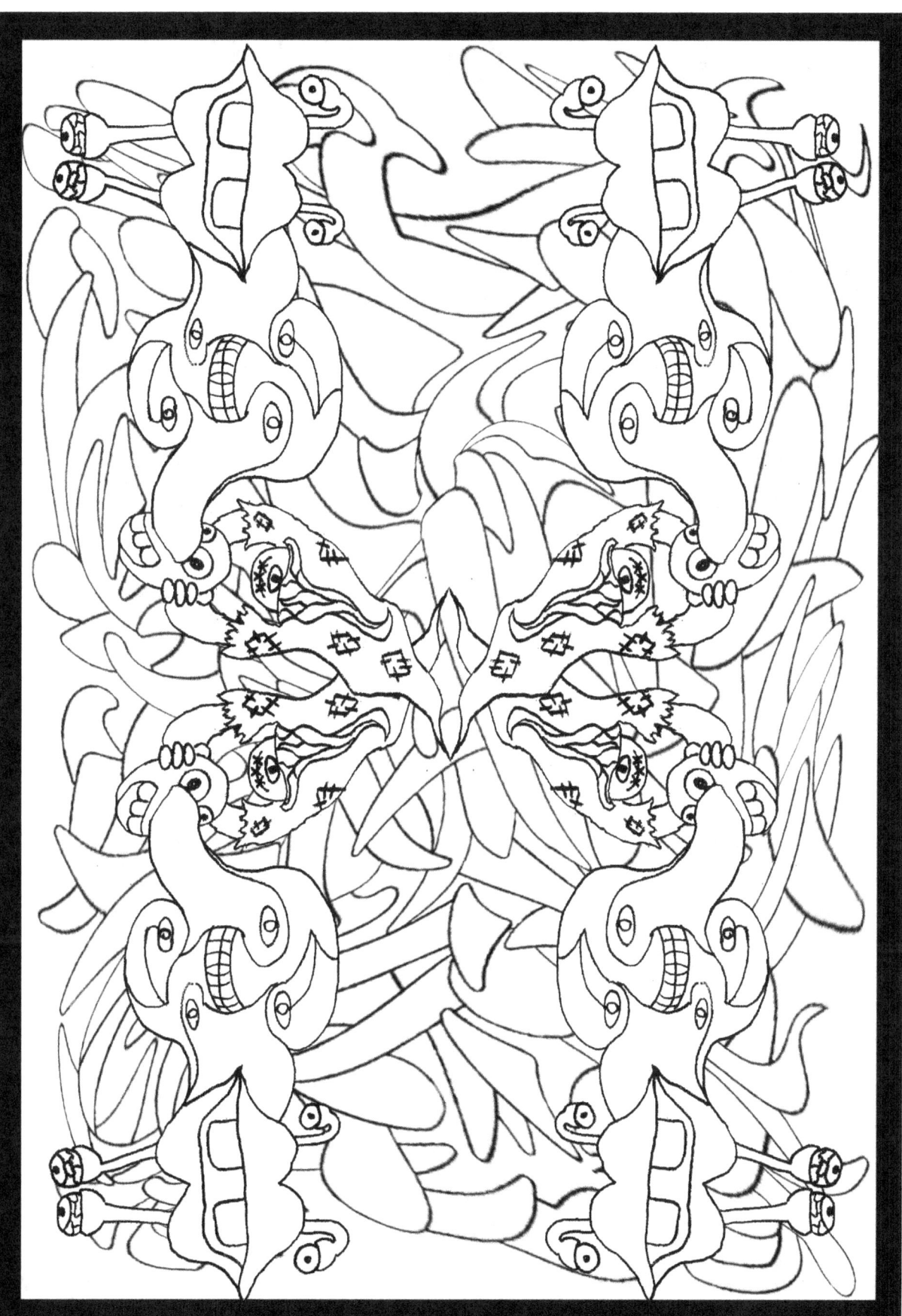

MONSTER REPORT

Monster Name:_____

Originates From:_____

Diet:_____

Description:_____

_____

_____

_____

_____

_____

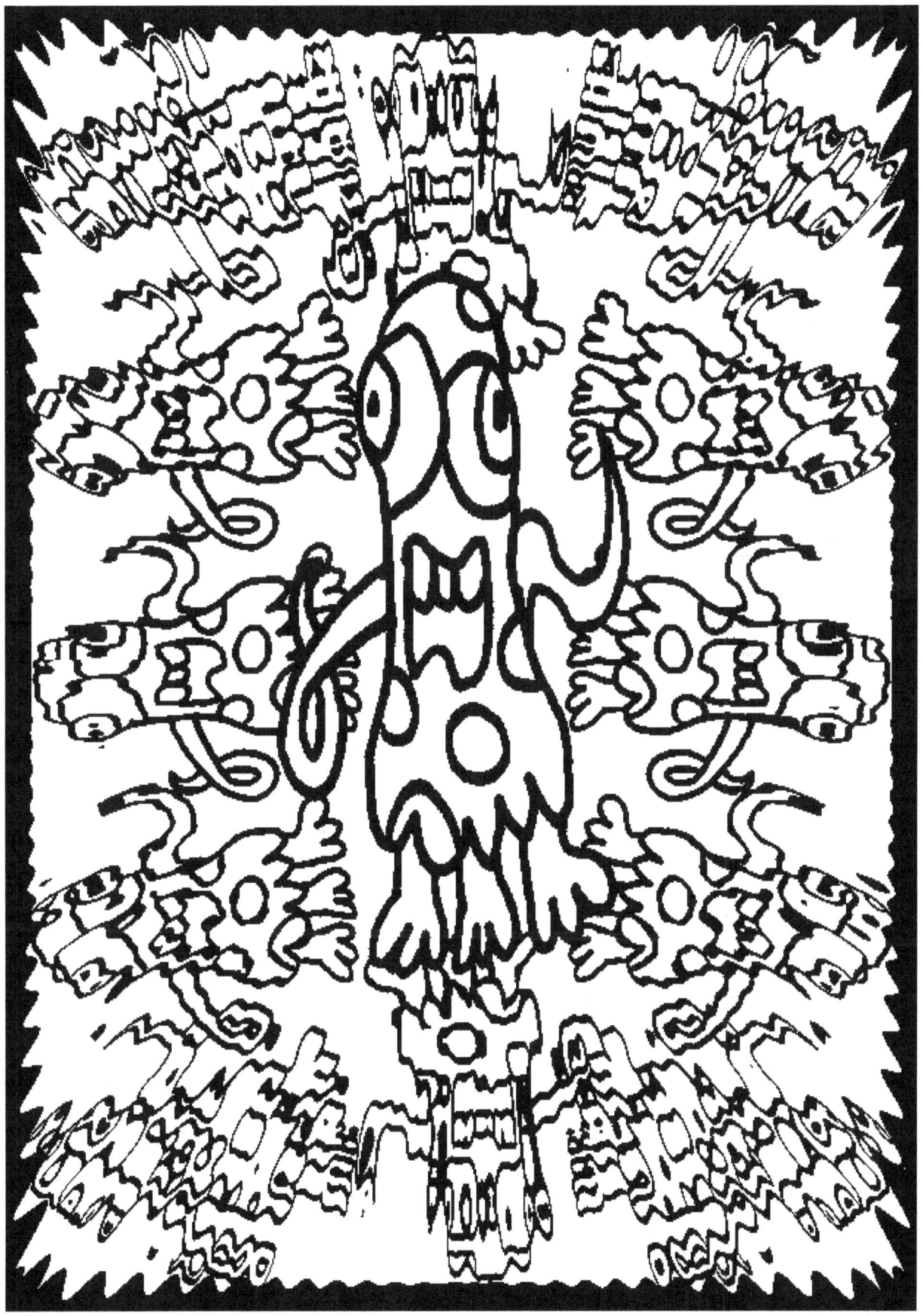

MONSTER REPORT

Monster Name:_____

Originates From:_____

Diet:_____

Description:_____

_____

_____

_____

_____

_____

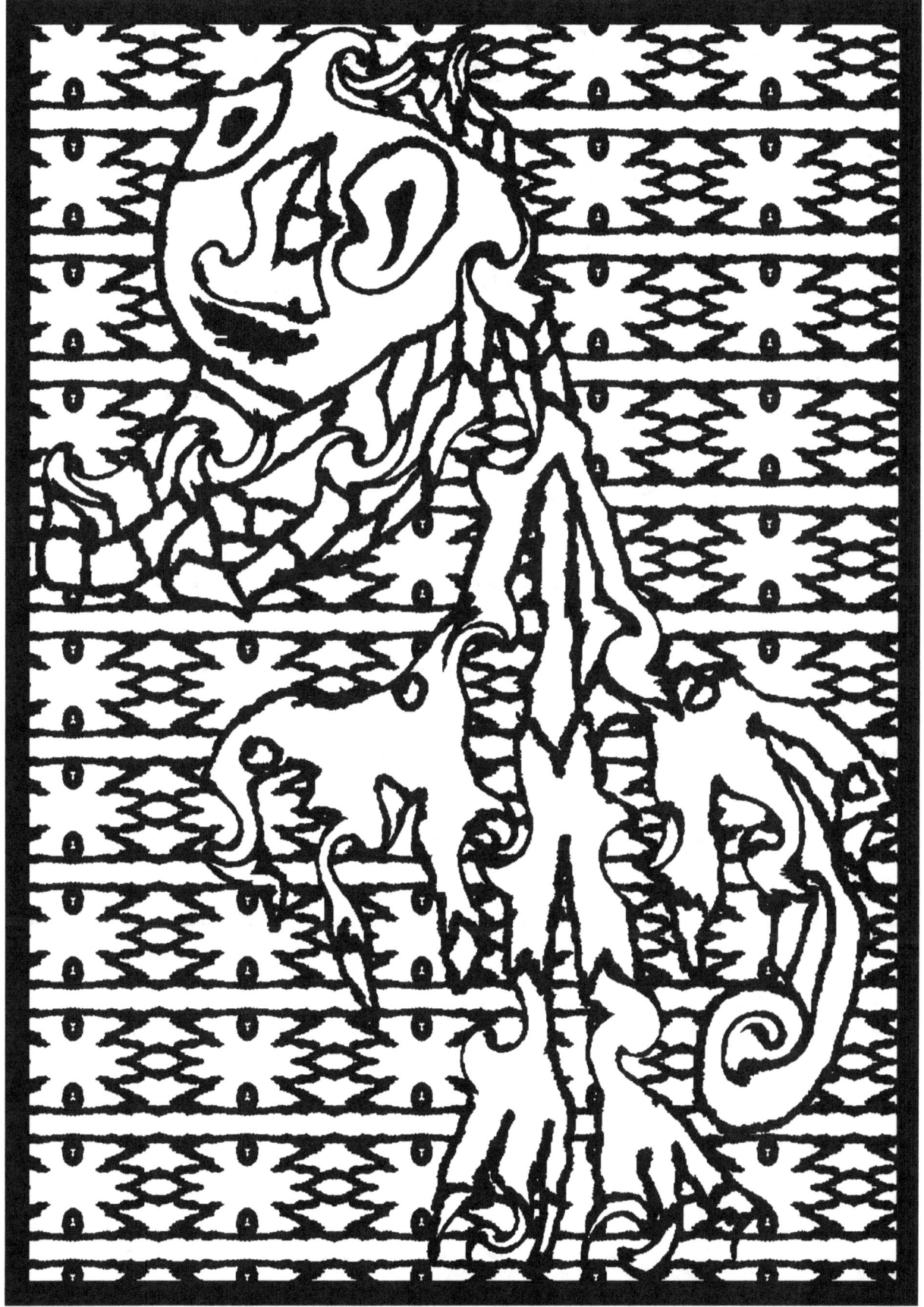

MONSTER REPORT

Monster Name:_____

Originates From:_____

Diet:_____

Description:_____

_____

_____

_____

_____

_____

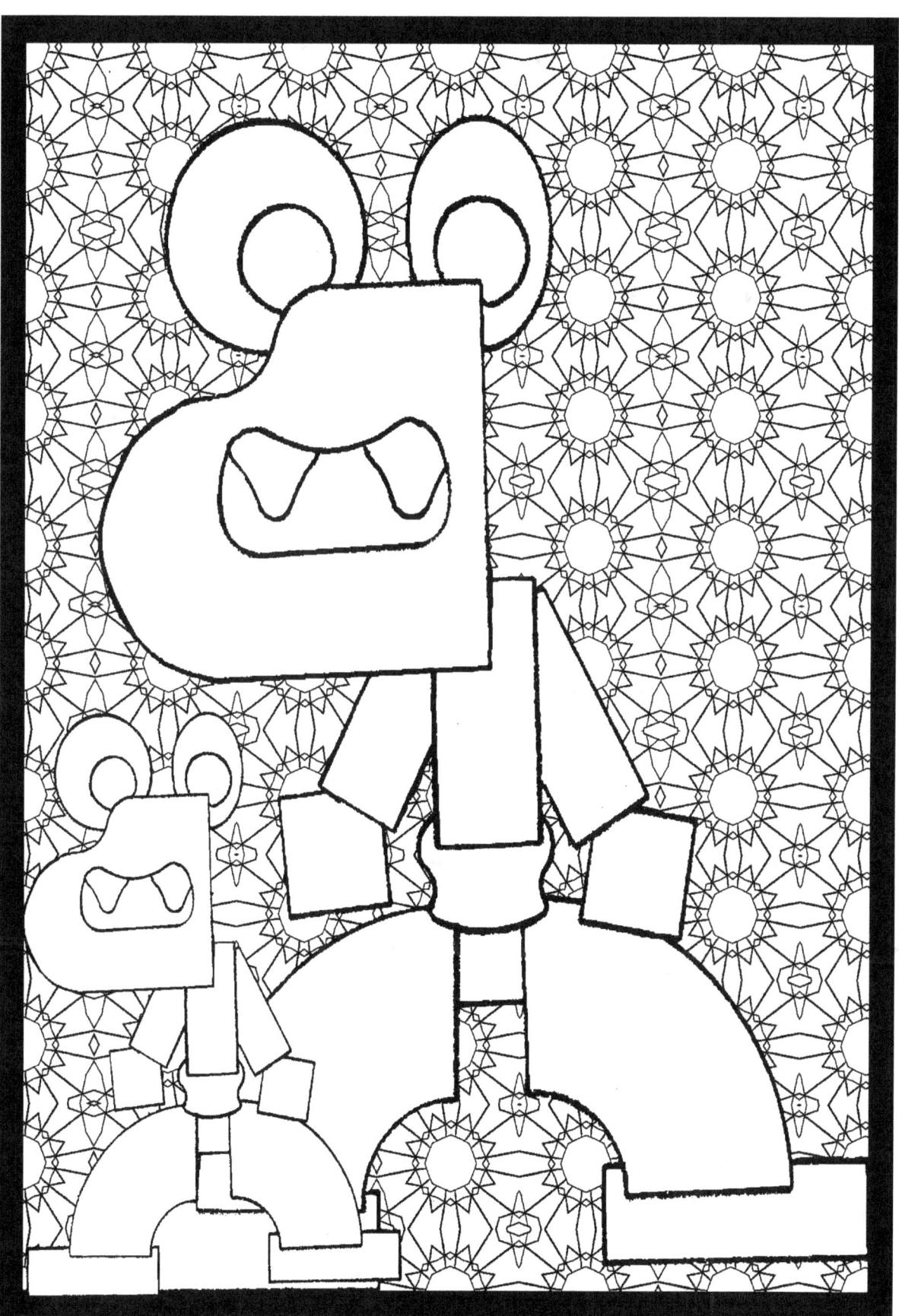

MONSTER REPORT

Monster Name:_____

Originates From:_____

Diet:_____

Description:_____

_____

_____

_____

_____

_____

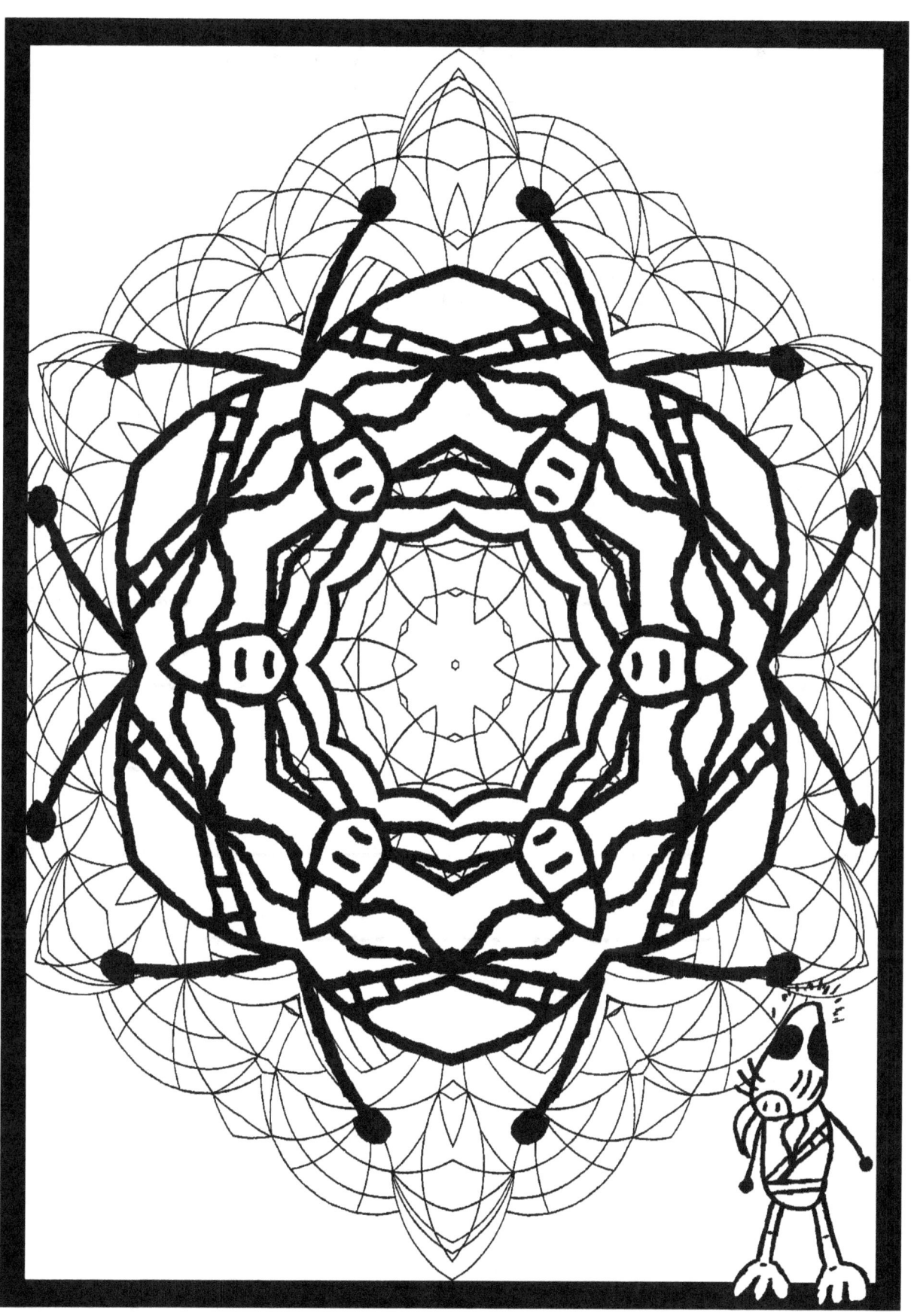

MONSTER REPORT

Monster Name:_____

Originates From:_____

Diet:_____

Description:_____

_____

_____

_____

_____

_____

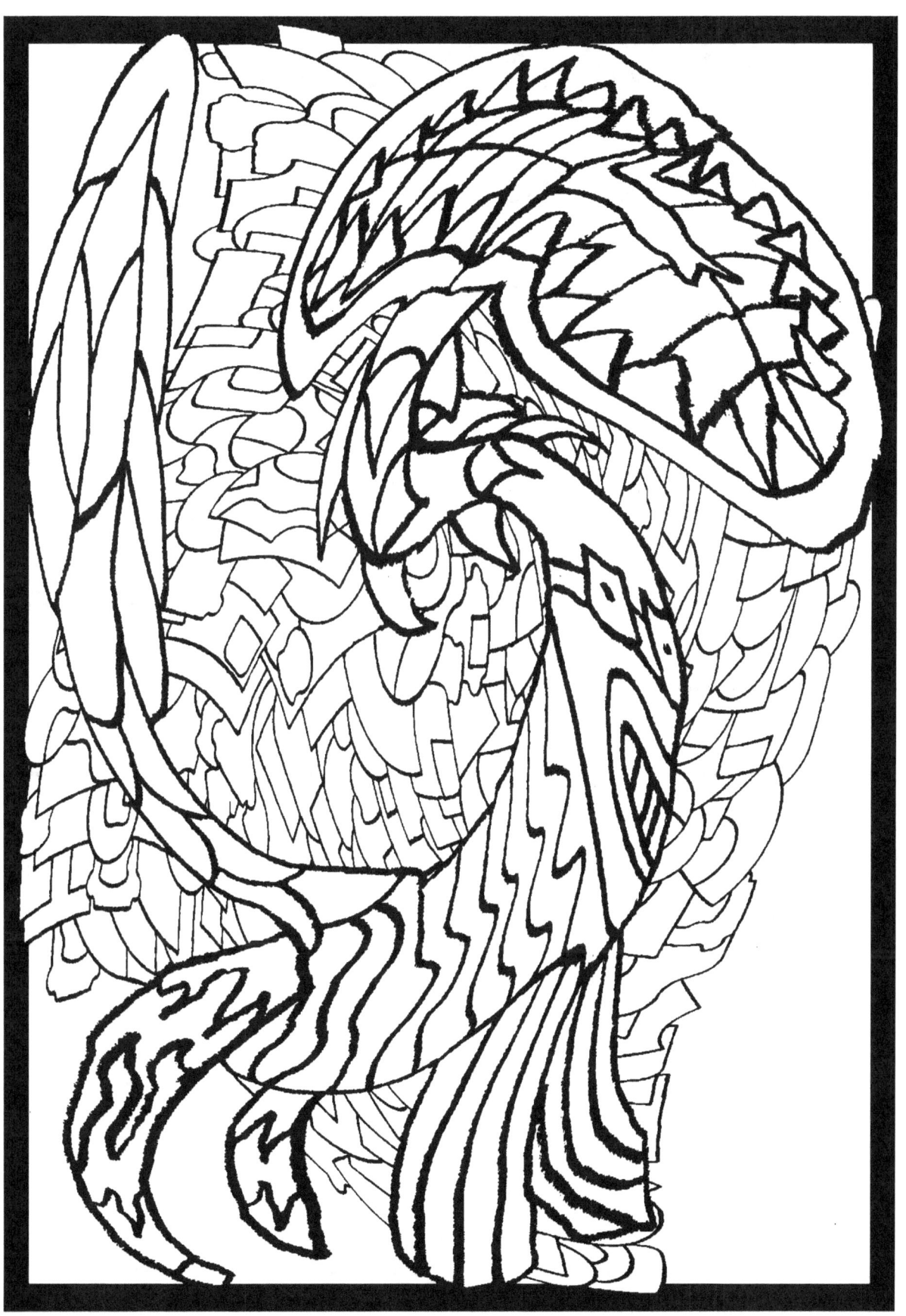

MONSTER REPORT

Monster Name:_____

Originates From:_____

Diet:_____

Description:_____

_____

_____

_____

_____

_____

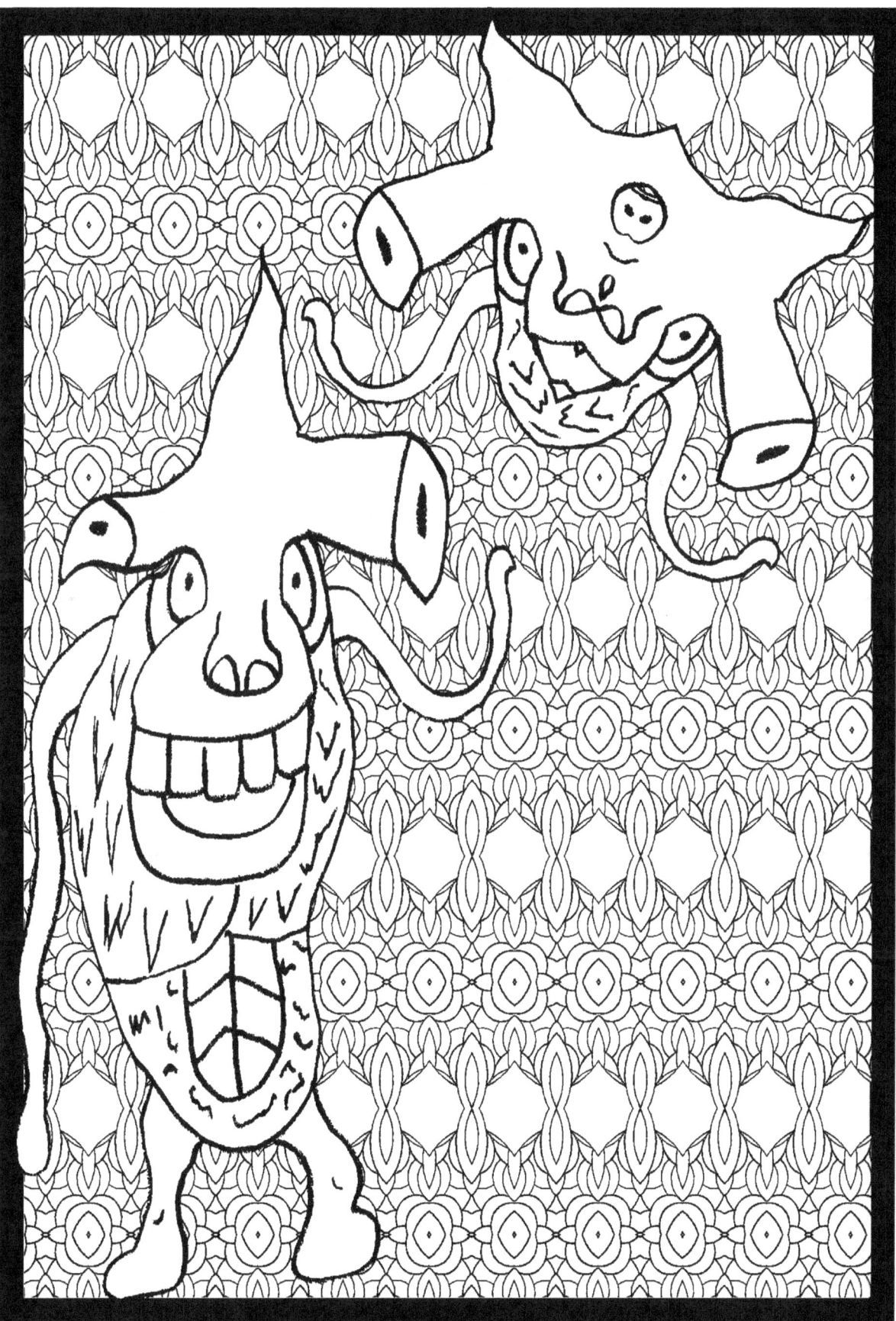

MONSTER REPORT

Monster Name:_____

Originates From:_____

Diet:_____

Description:_____

_____

_____

_____

_____

_____

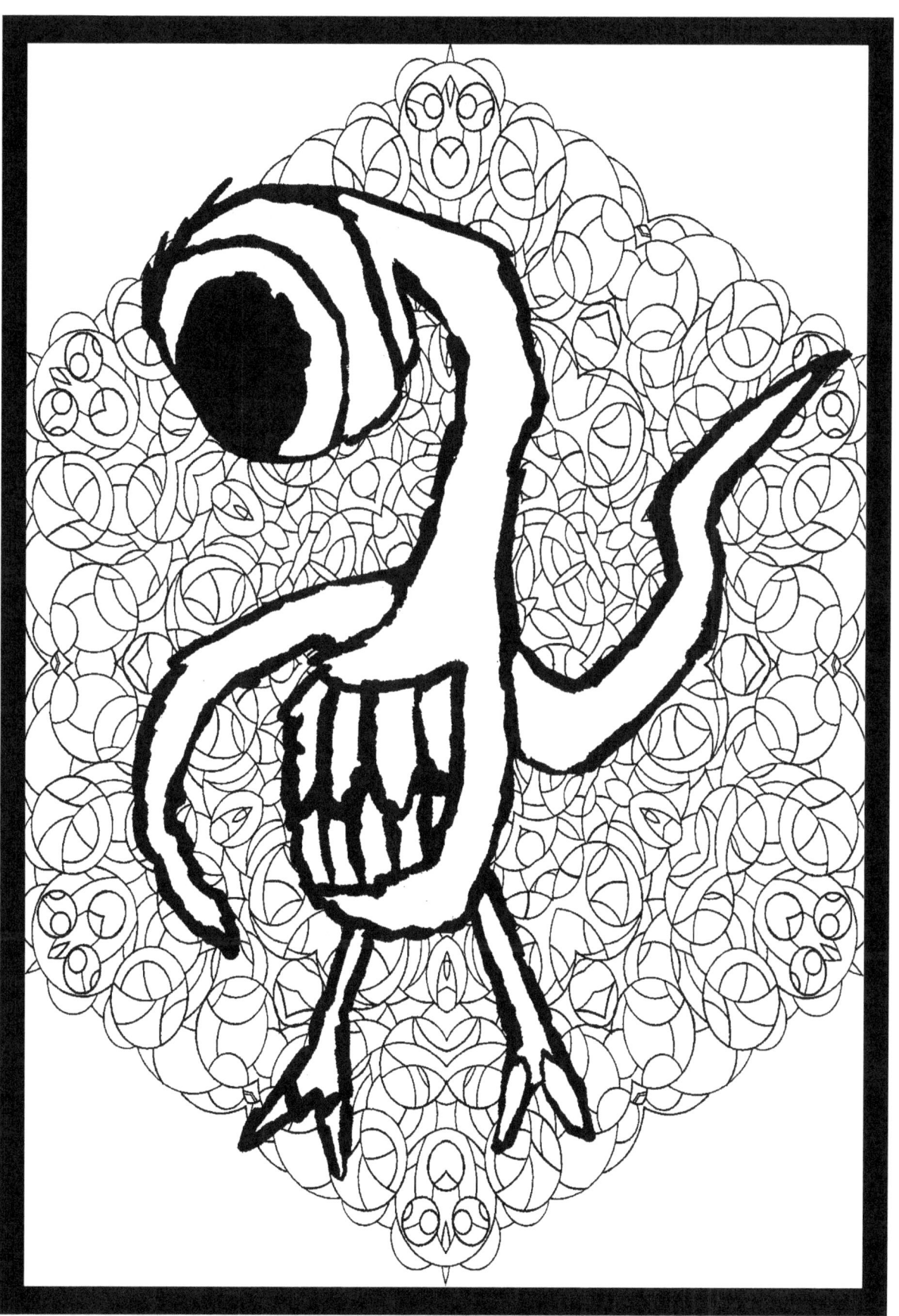

You've made it to the end! Congratulations and thanks for coloring!

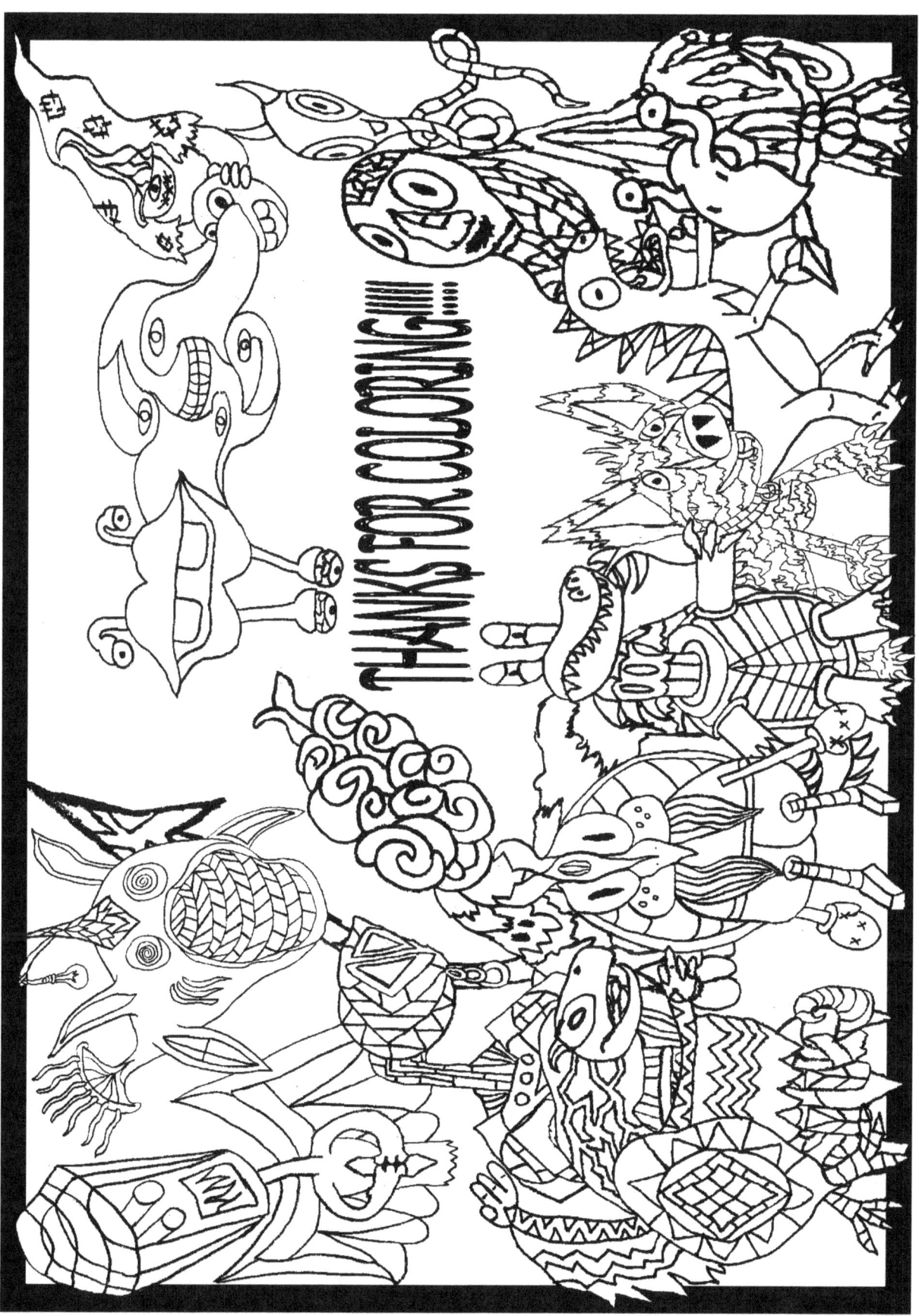

Bonus Pages Approaching!!!

These were pages I made playing around with my random tools in my editing software and I thought were cool to add. A lot of them are the same monsters but with twists to their prior appearances. Either way, they are meant for you to have even more fun with my creations. Enjoy!

One of my personal favorites (kind of why it's the cover image).

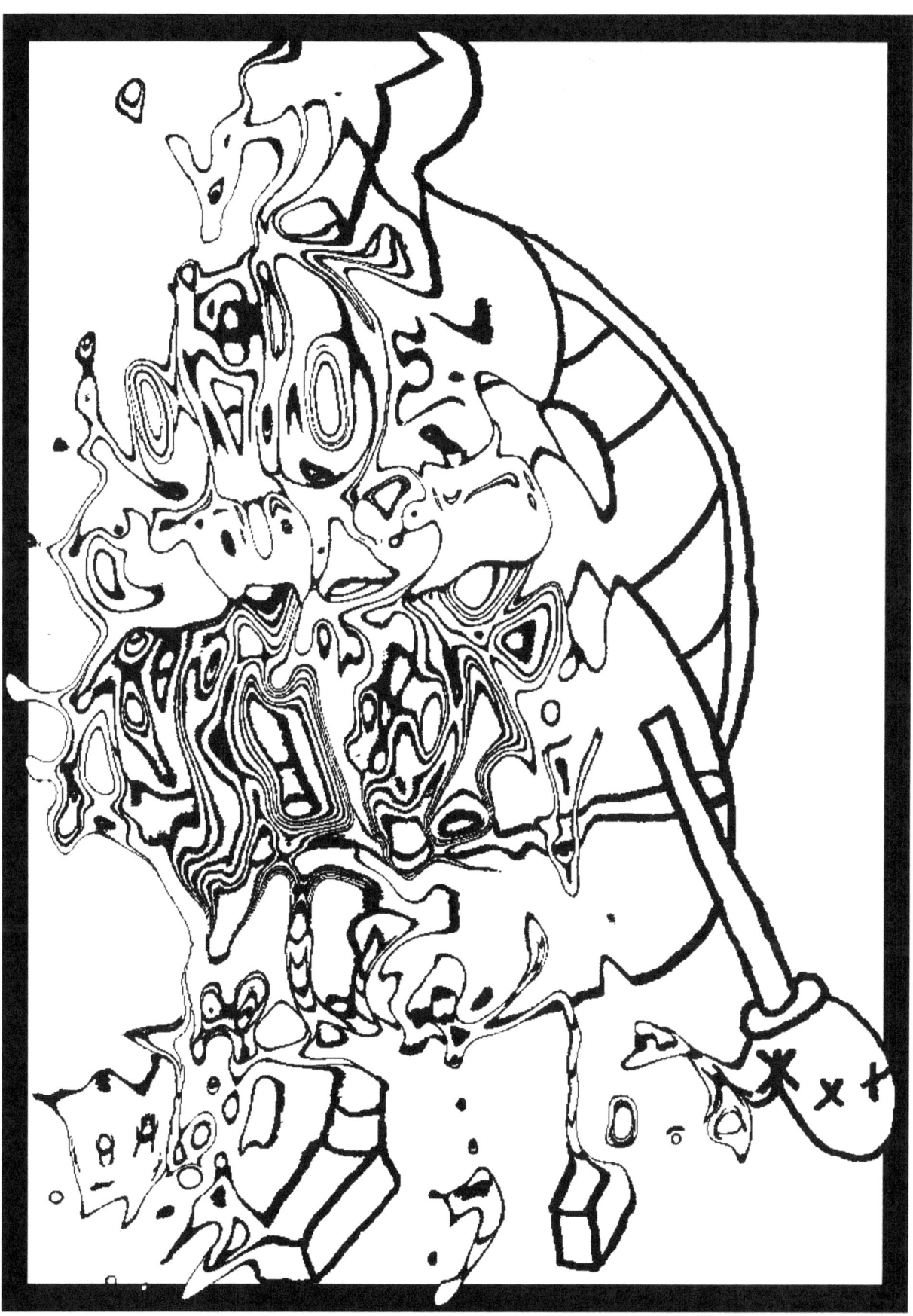

Playing with distortion.

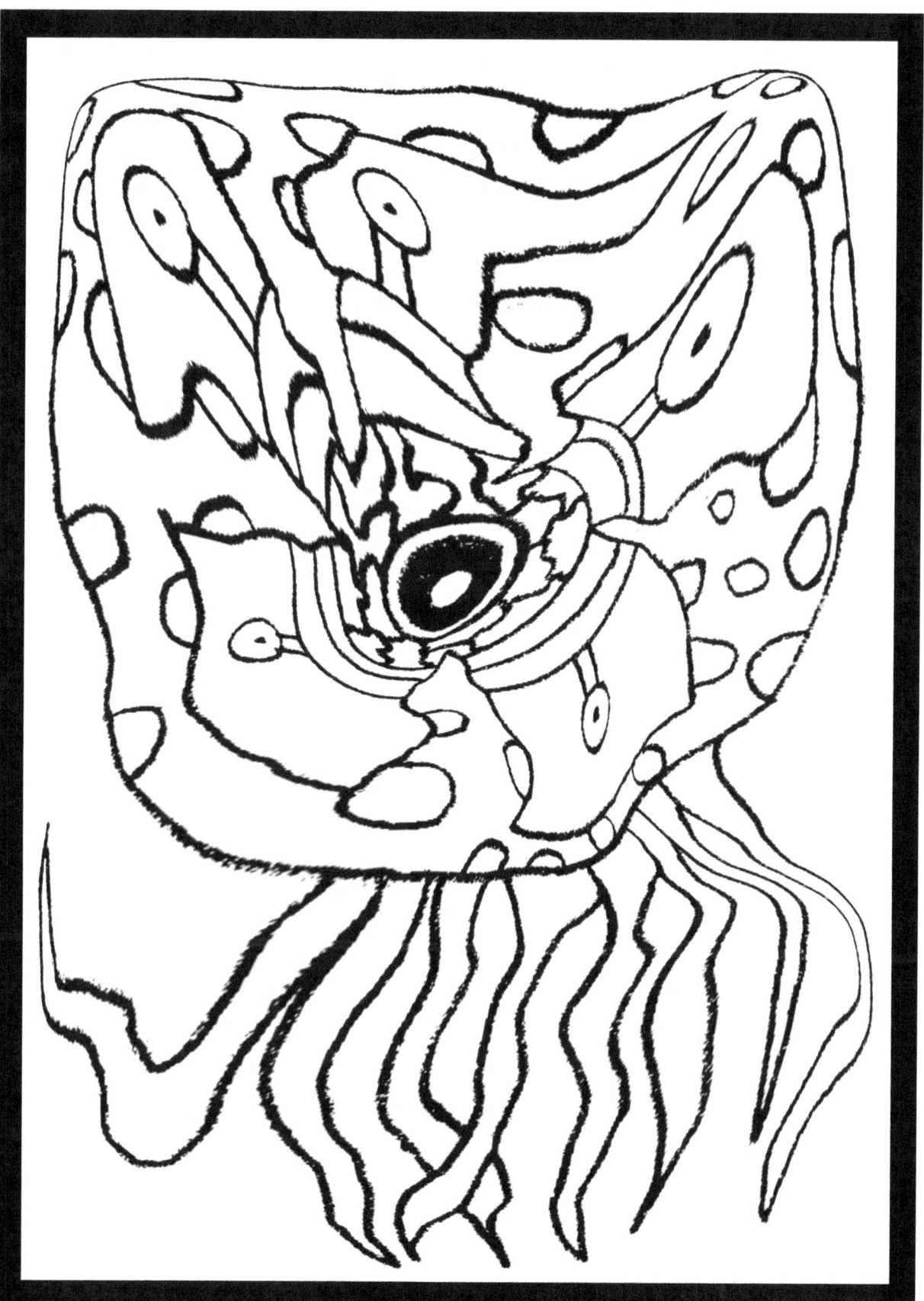

Reminds me of either film reels or comic panels.

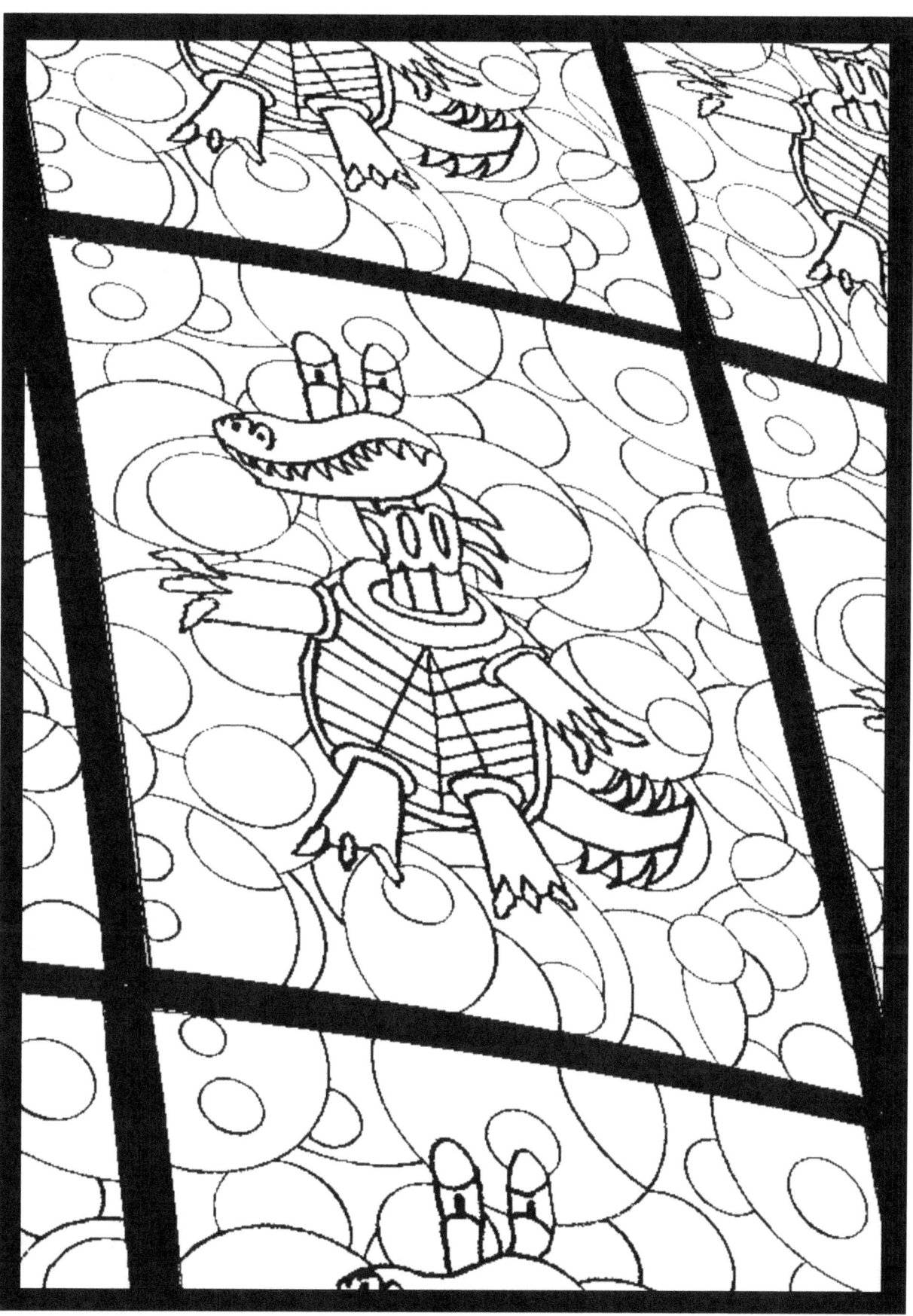

This was way too plain this way for the main section. I still wanted to include this creep though.

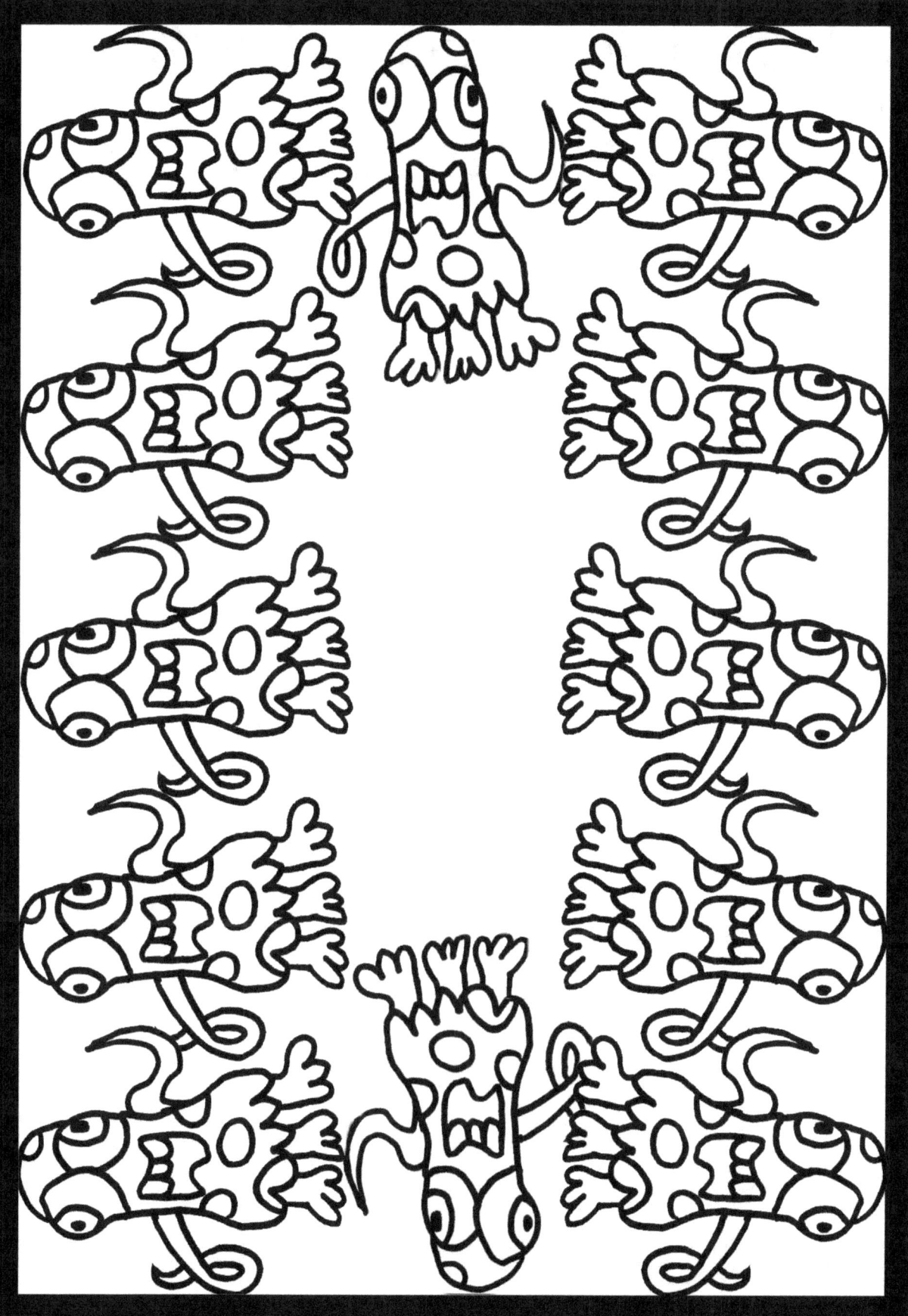

Not twisted like the
one featured early.

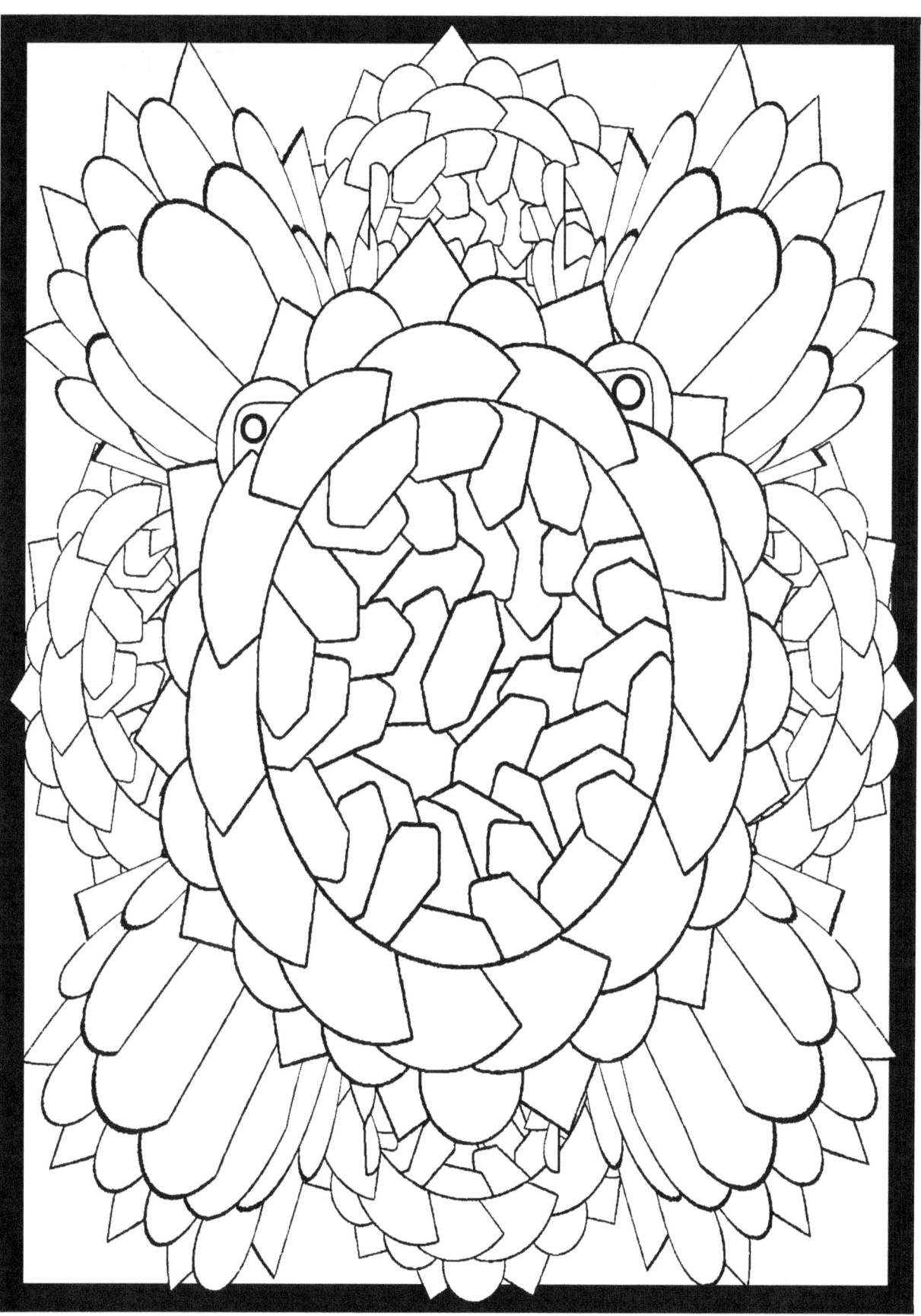

Personally as the artist behind this guy, I really have a love/hate relationship with him. He looks neat but finding ways of what to do with him took me a minute.

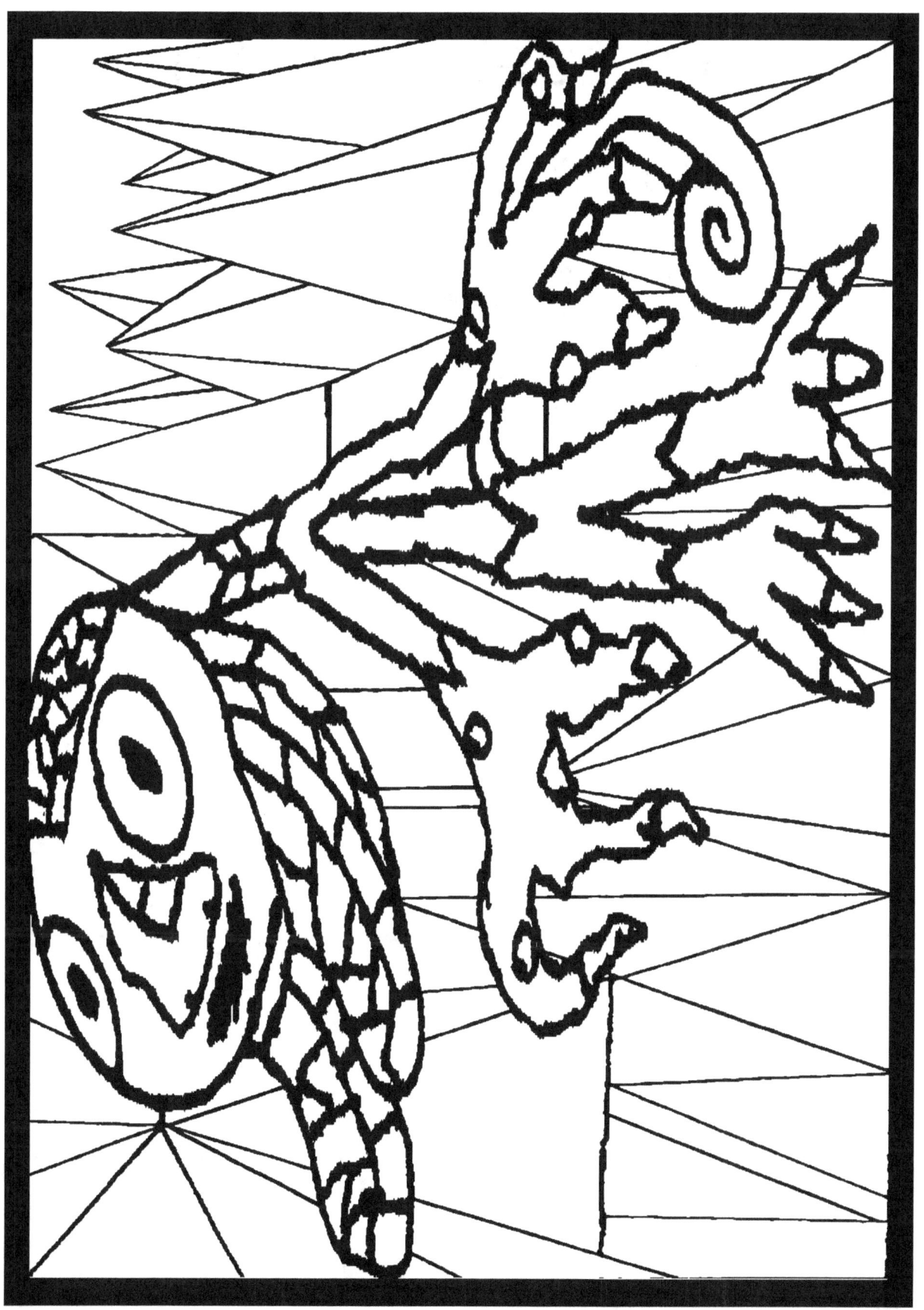

Pre fusion with another bot before their appearance in this publication.

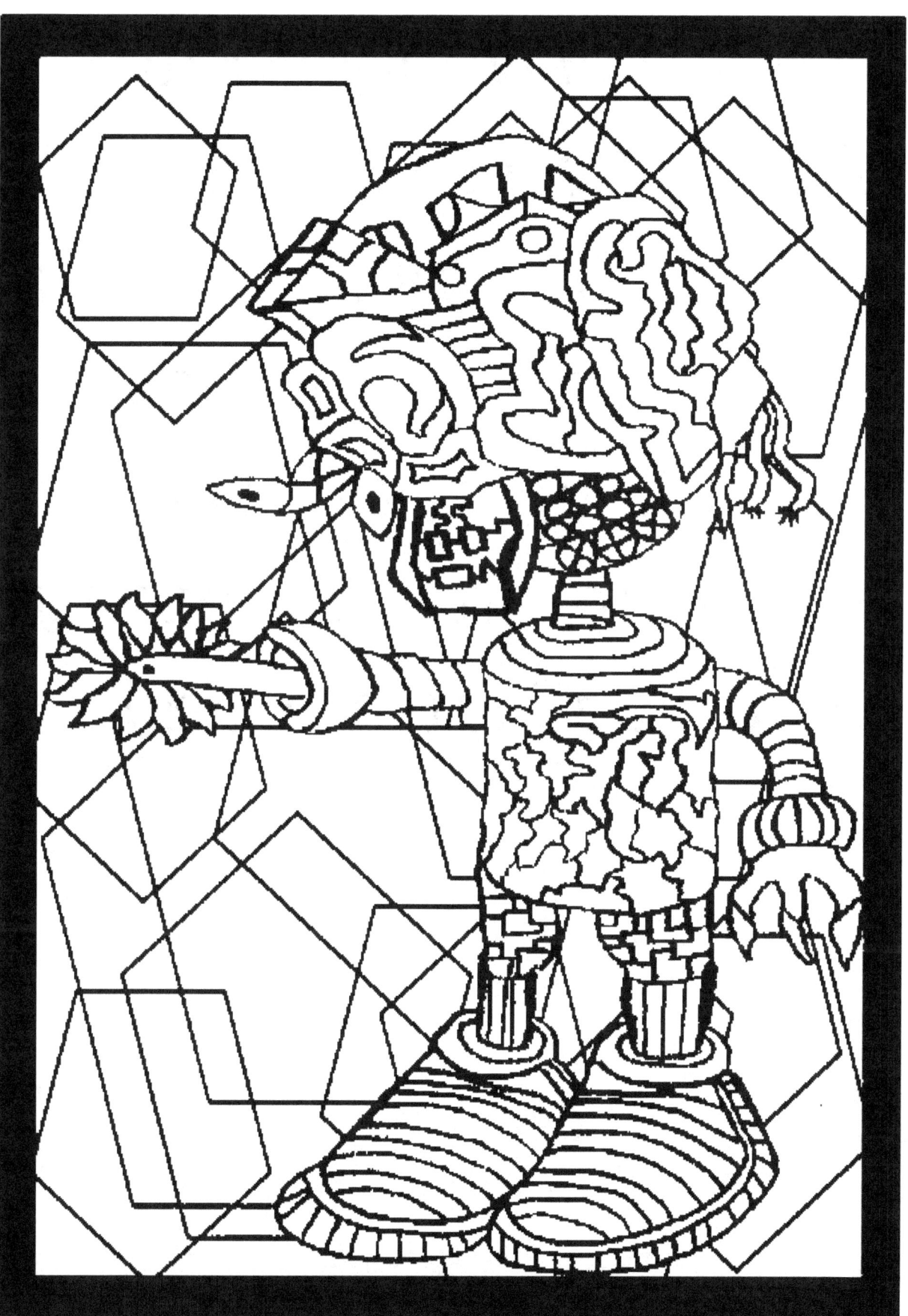

My other personal favorite is this gator and turtle hybrid. This is what he starts looking like after working on a coloring book after all day,

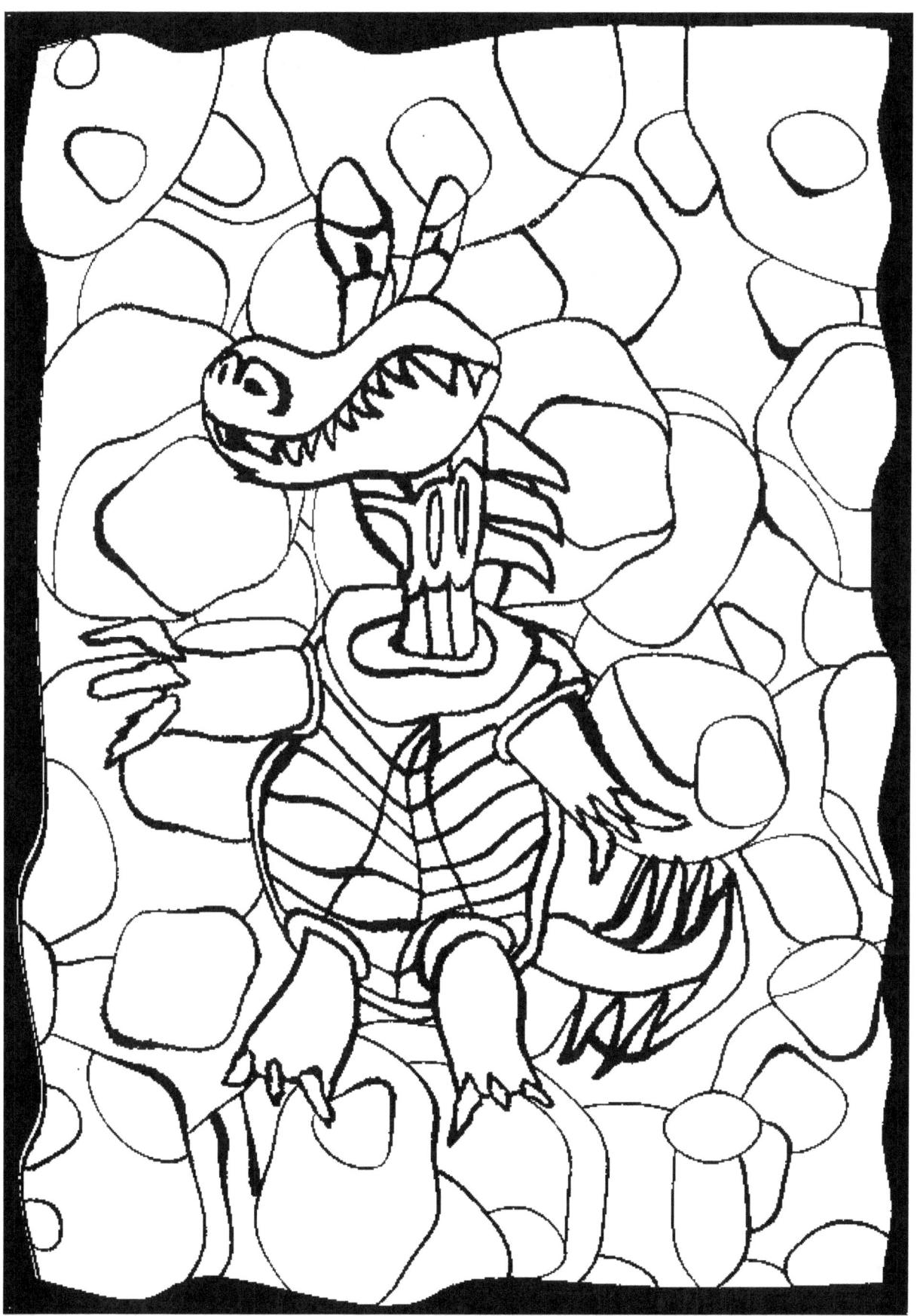

I really dig how these turn out when I kaleidoscope them.

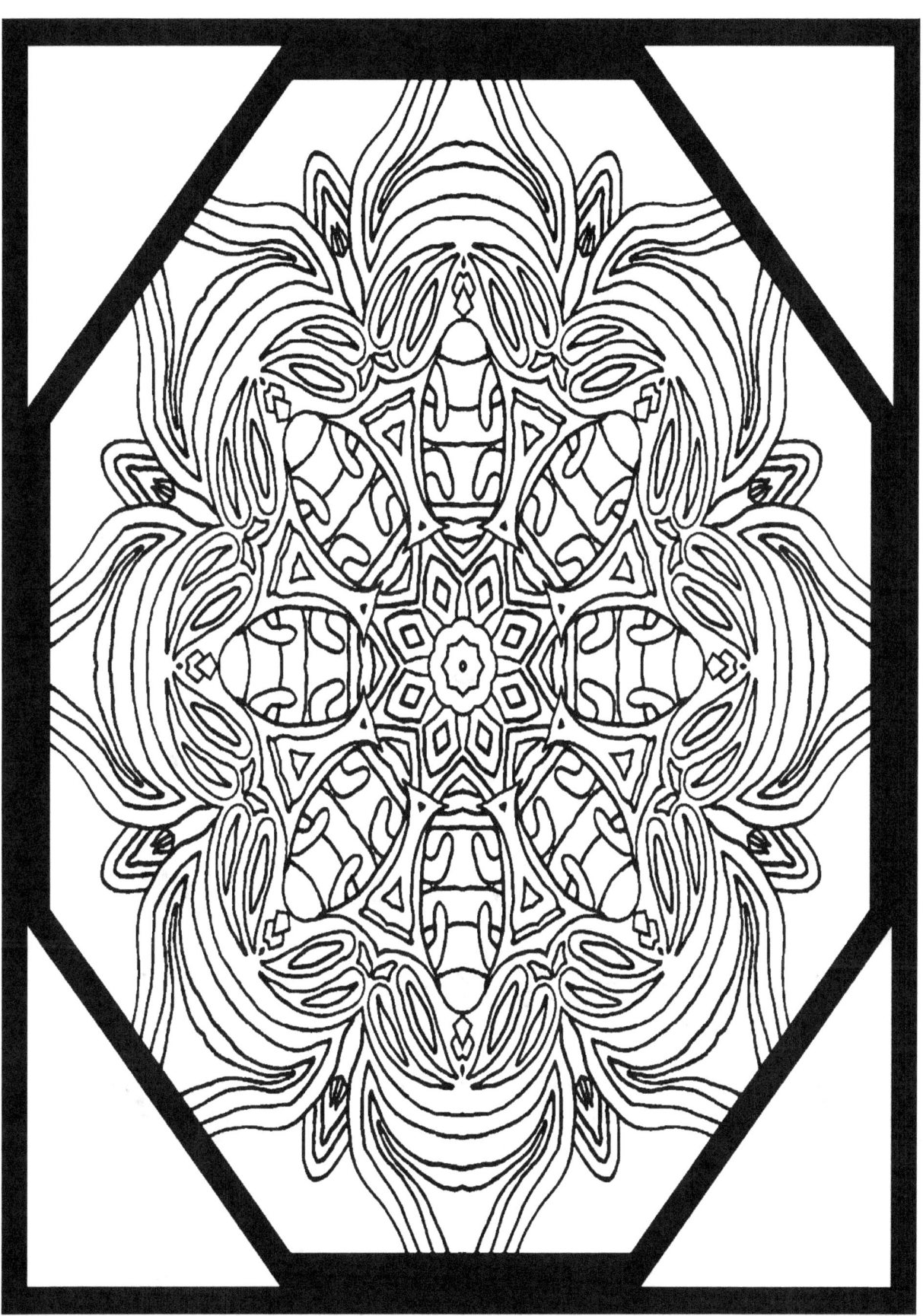

I honestly couldn't help but put a picture of a distorted Gatortle since I have one of Bearded Boxer as the cover. Author note; these two are my favorite monsters I made for this book.

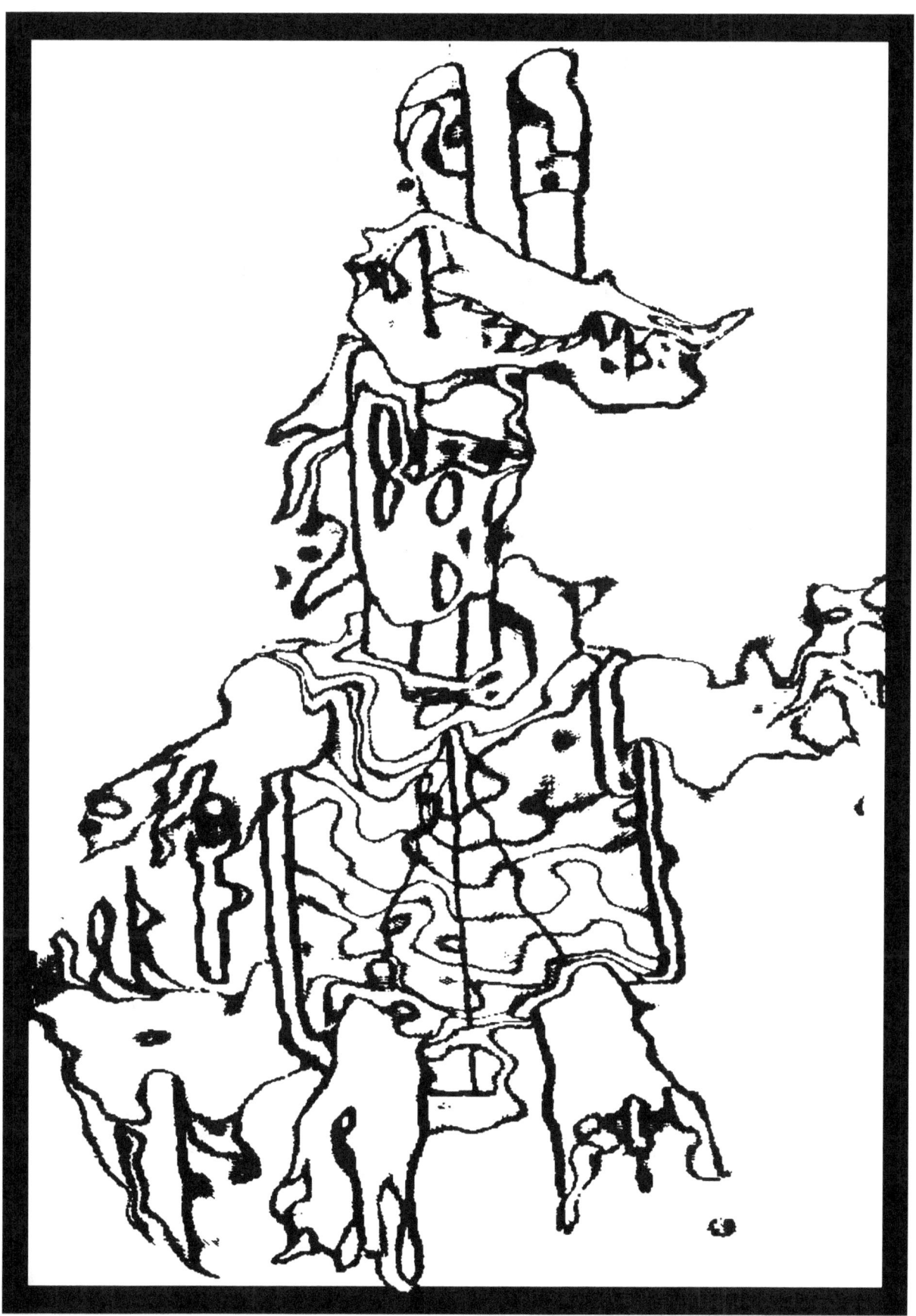

I really just like adding in bonus pages for you readers.

Maybe if I didn't love you all so much.

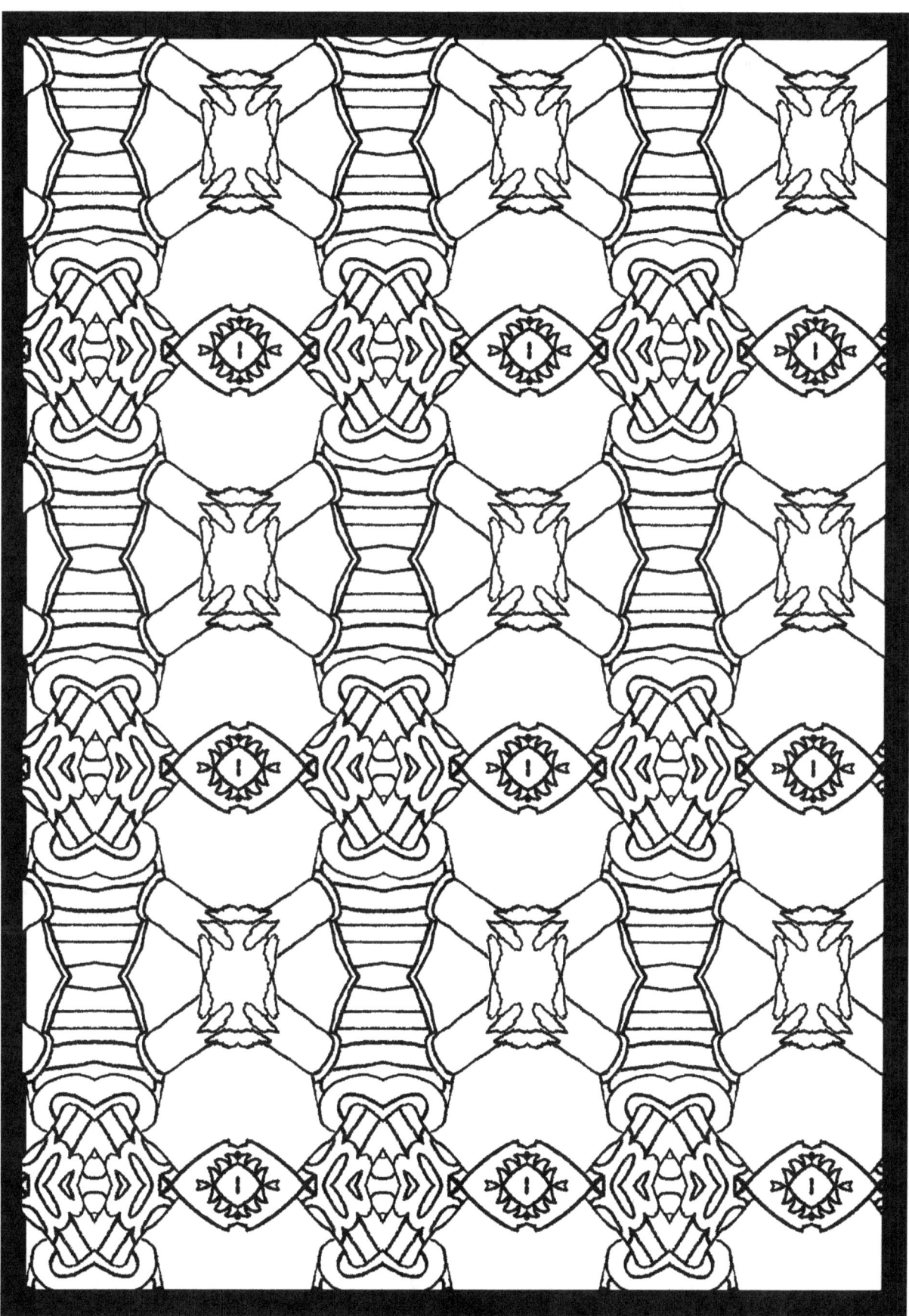

Watch the teeth!

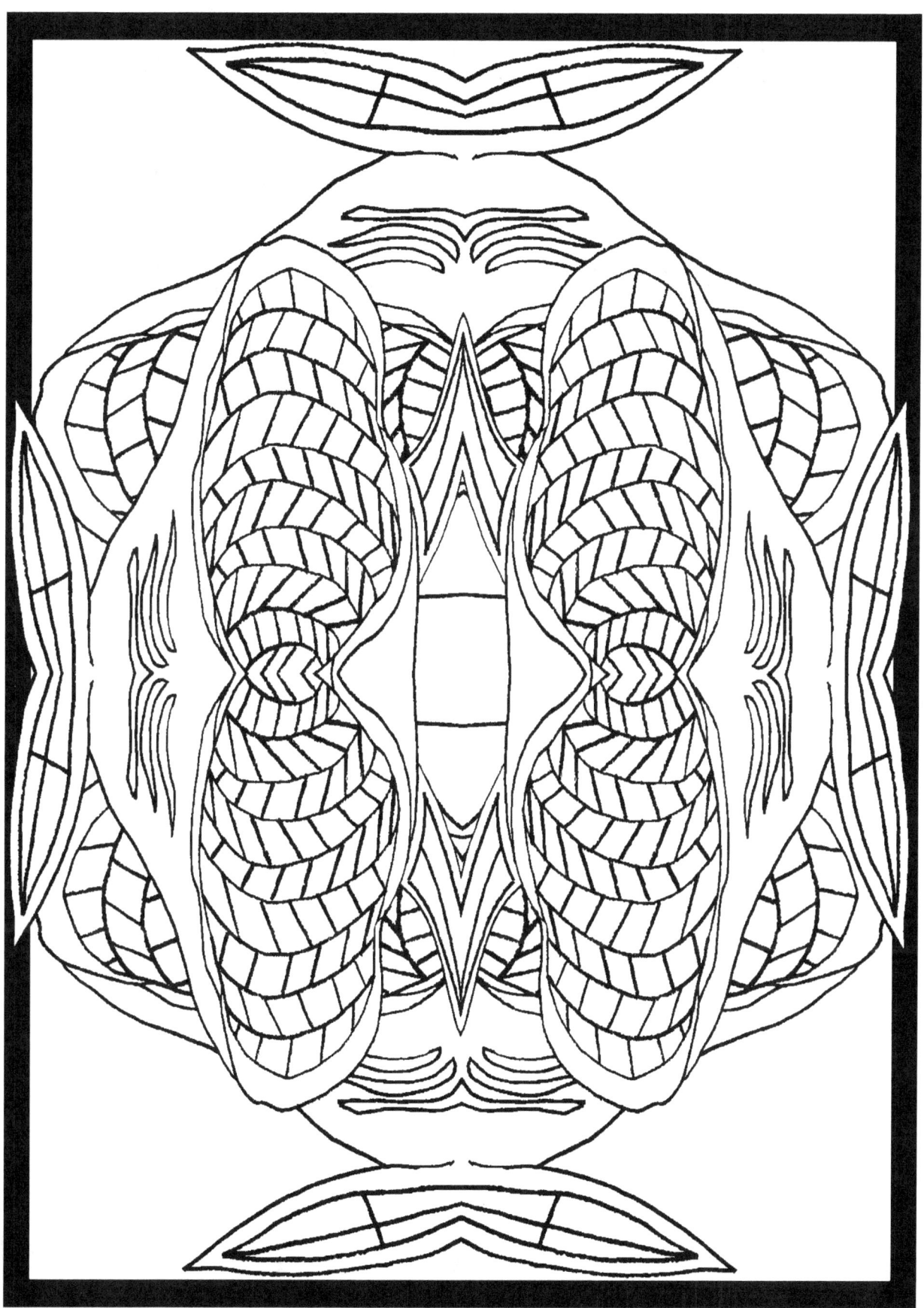

Because I clearly haven't done enough with this guy yet.

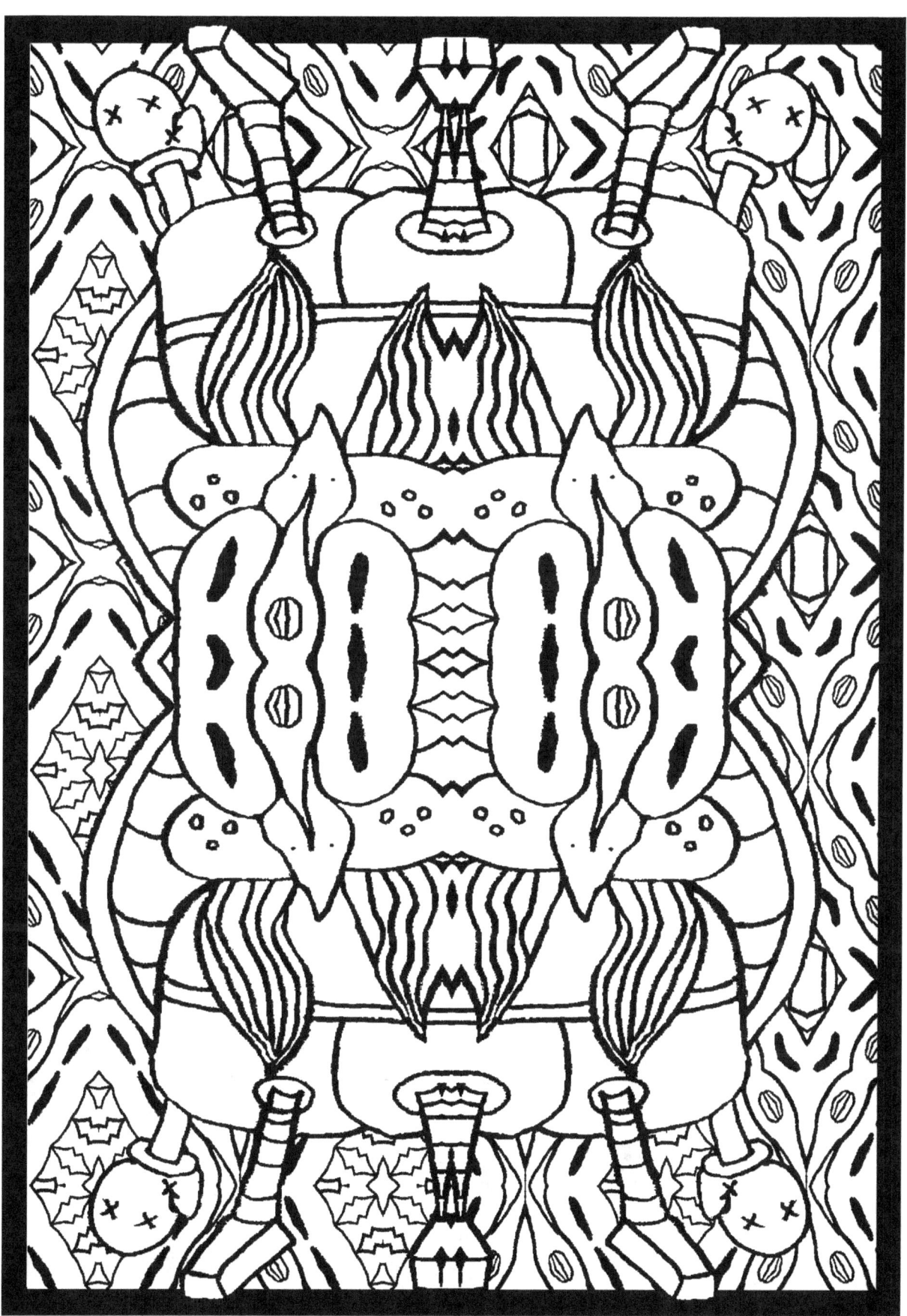

...

...

...

...

...

...

...

I'm not even sure, just
enjoy it...

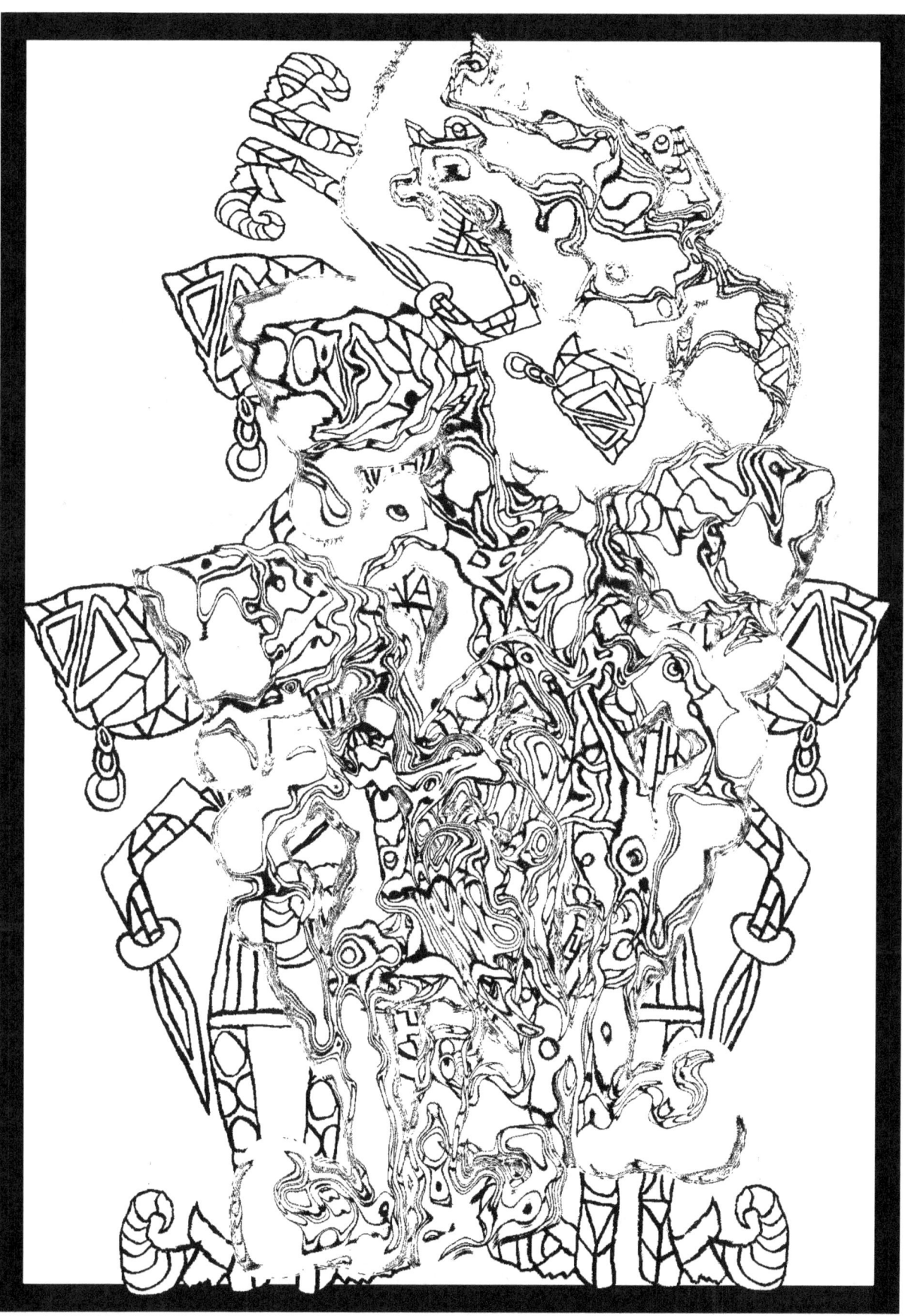

"That's all Folks!" Well, after a few more bouns pictures. This worm just reminds me of Porky Pig popping out of the screen.

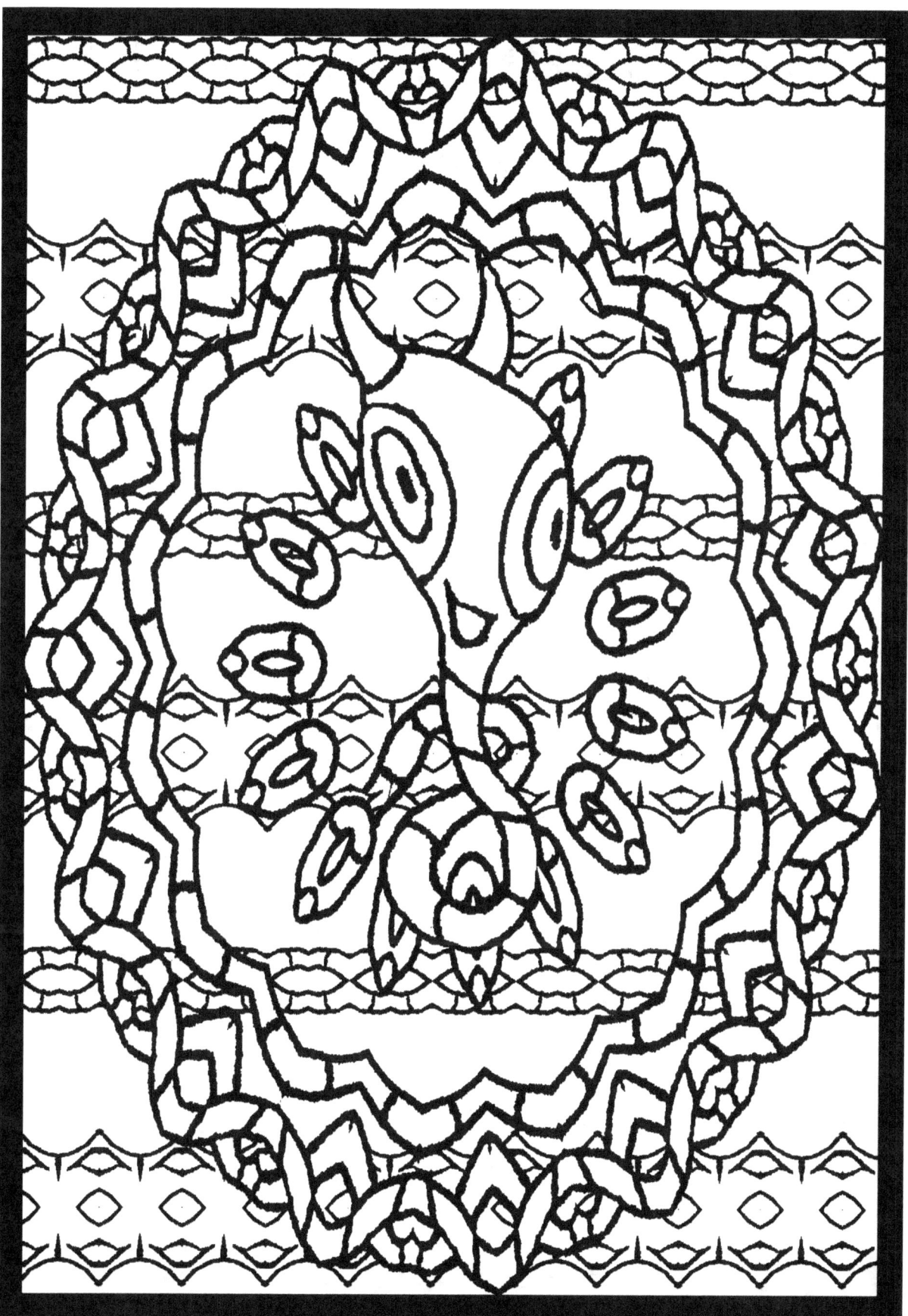

Glad this thing isn't real.

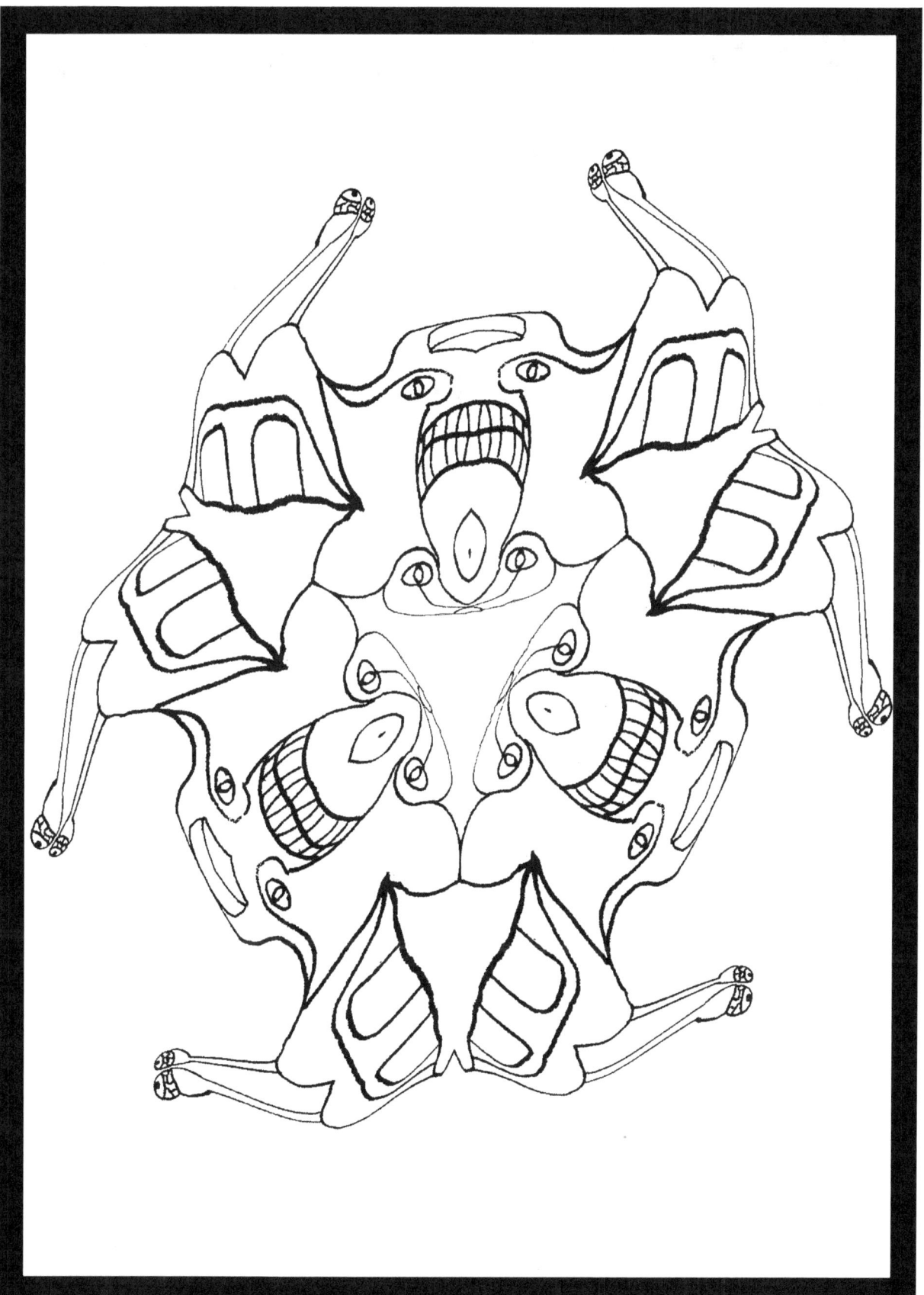

When it's really dark in the depths of the ocean and you need twice as much light.

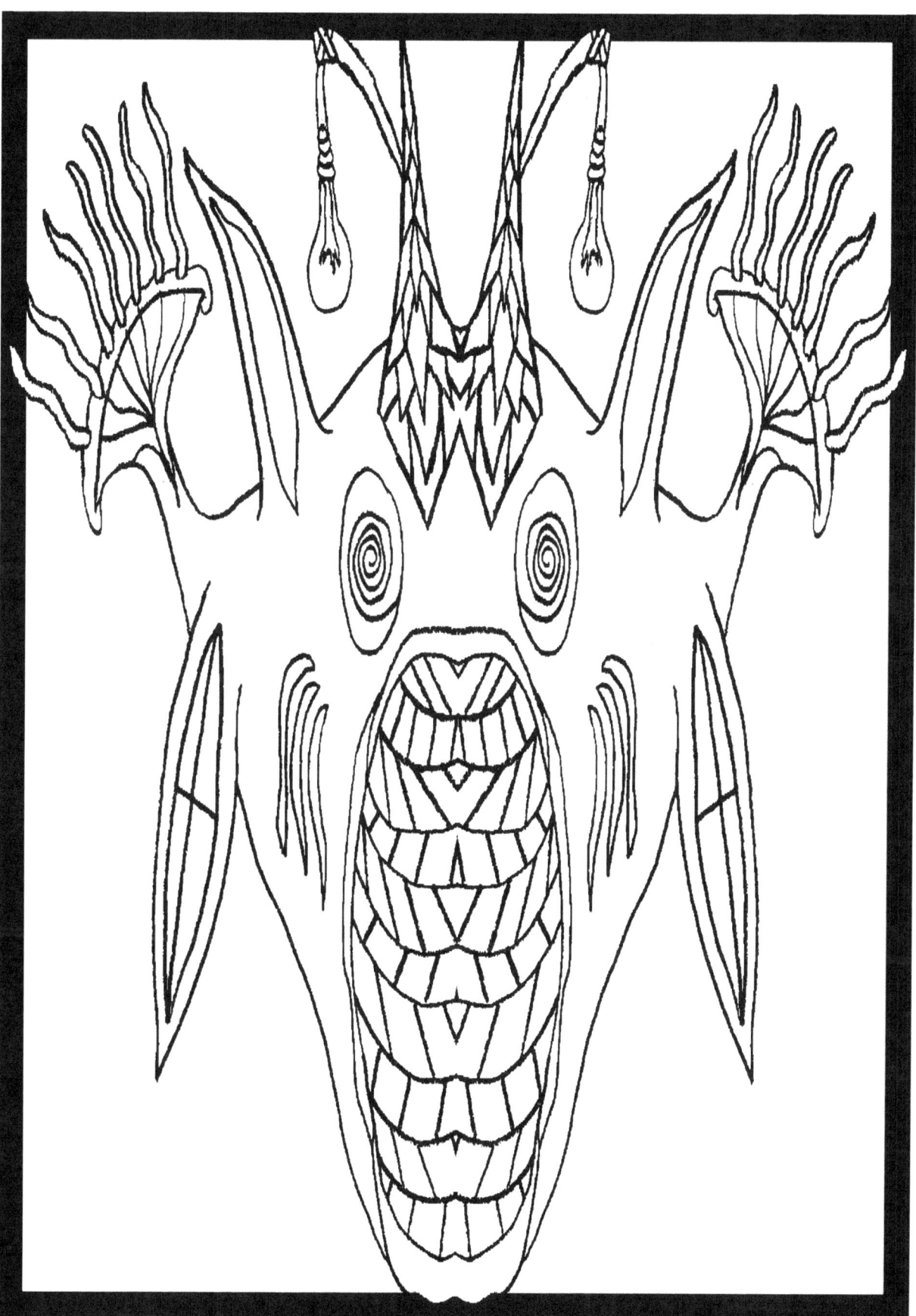

We might be losing control...

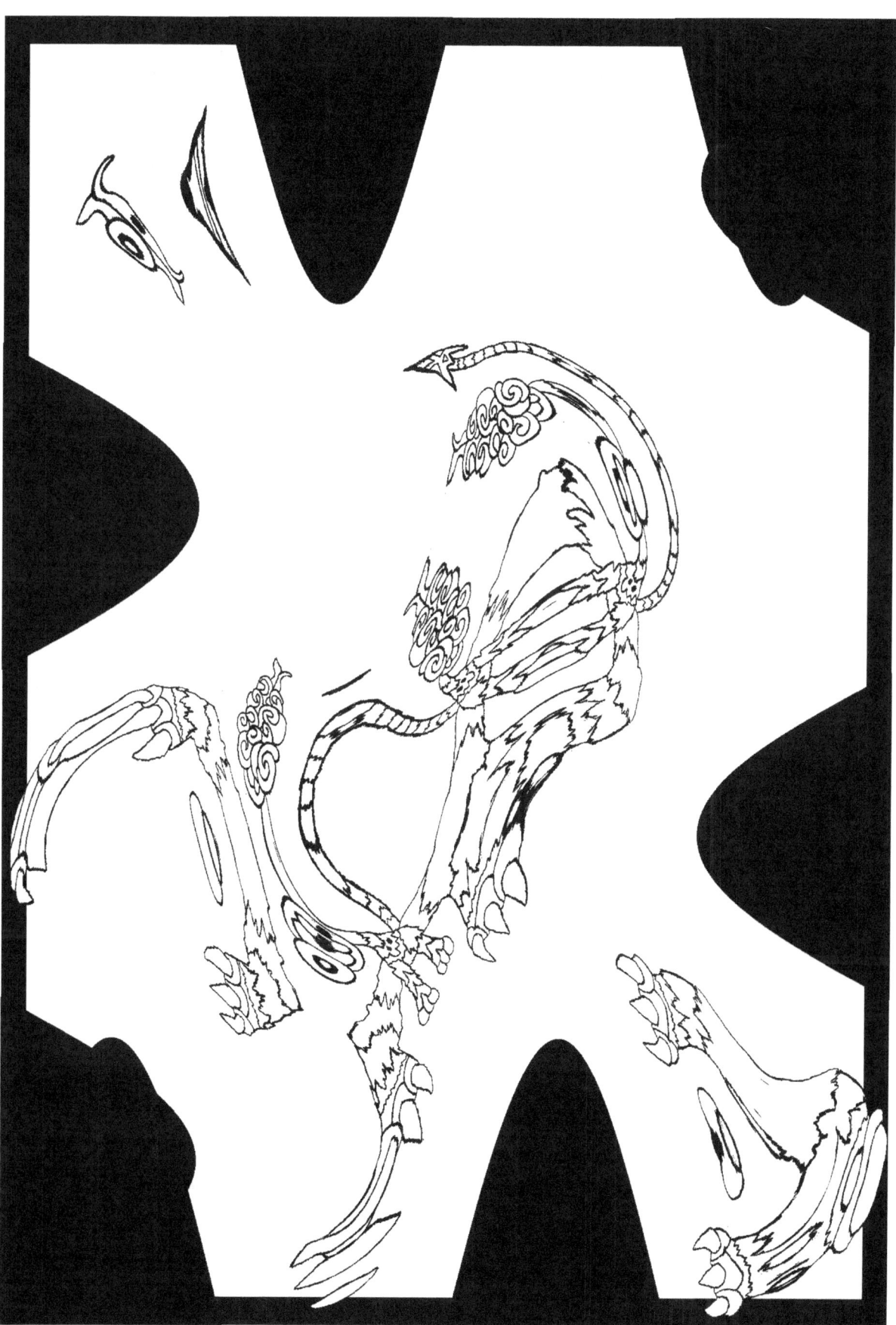

What are you so twisted out of shape for?

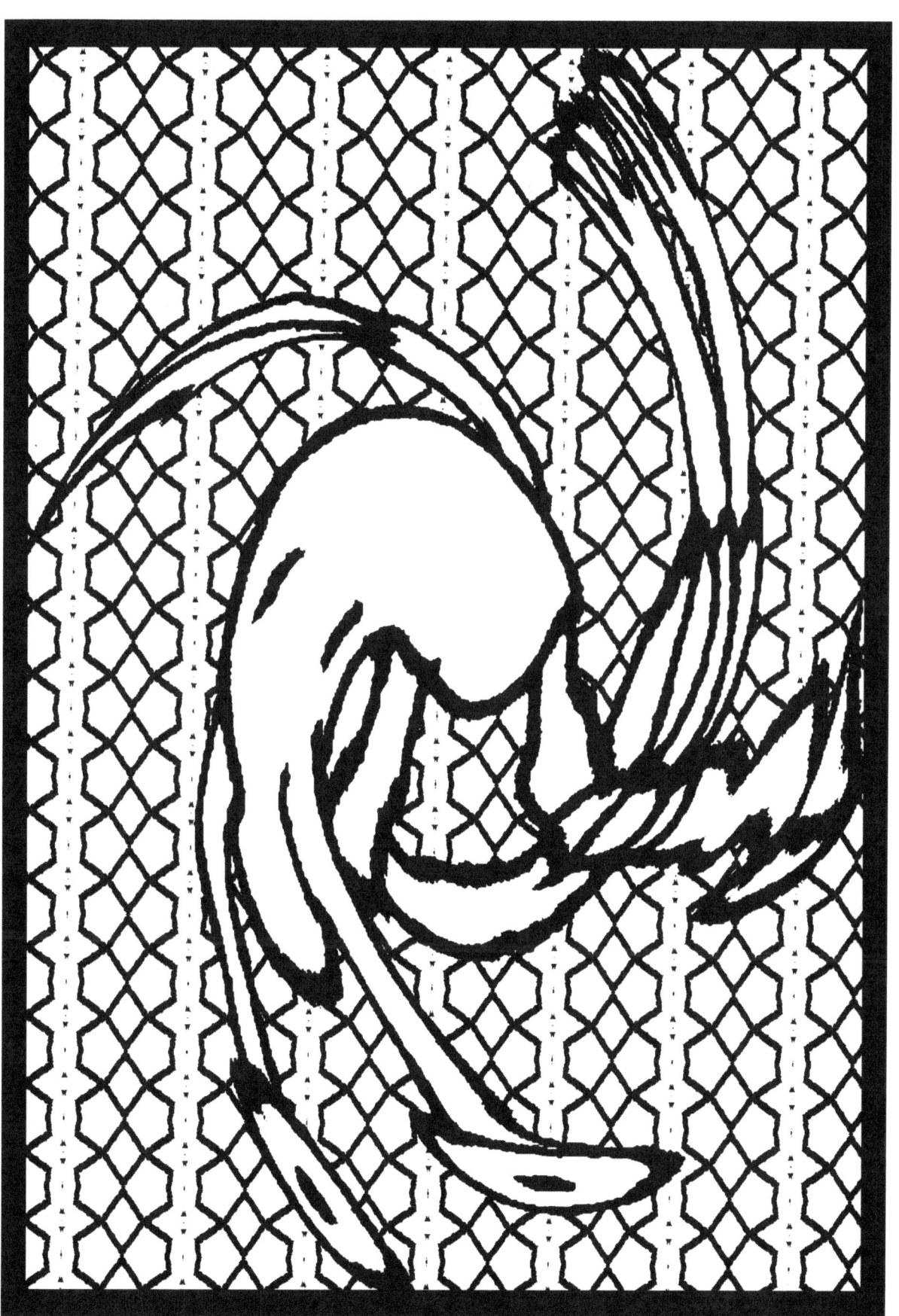

When kaleidescoping a monster makes it look like mages casting a spell in unison.

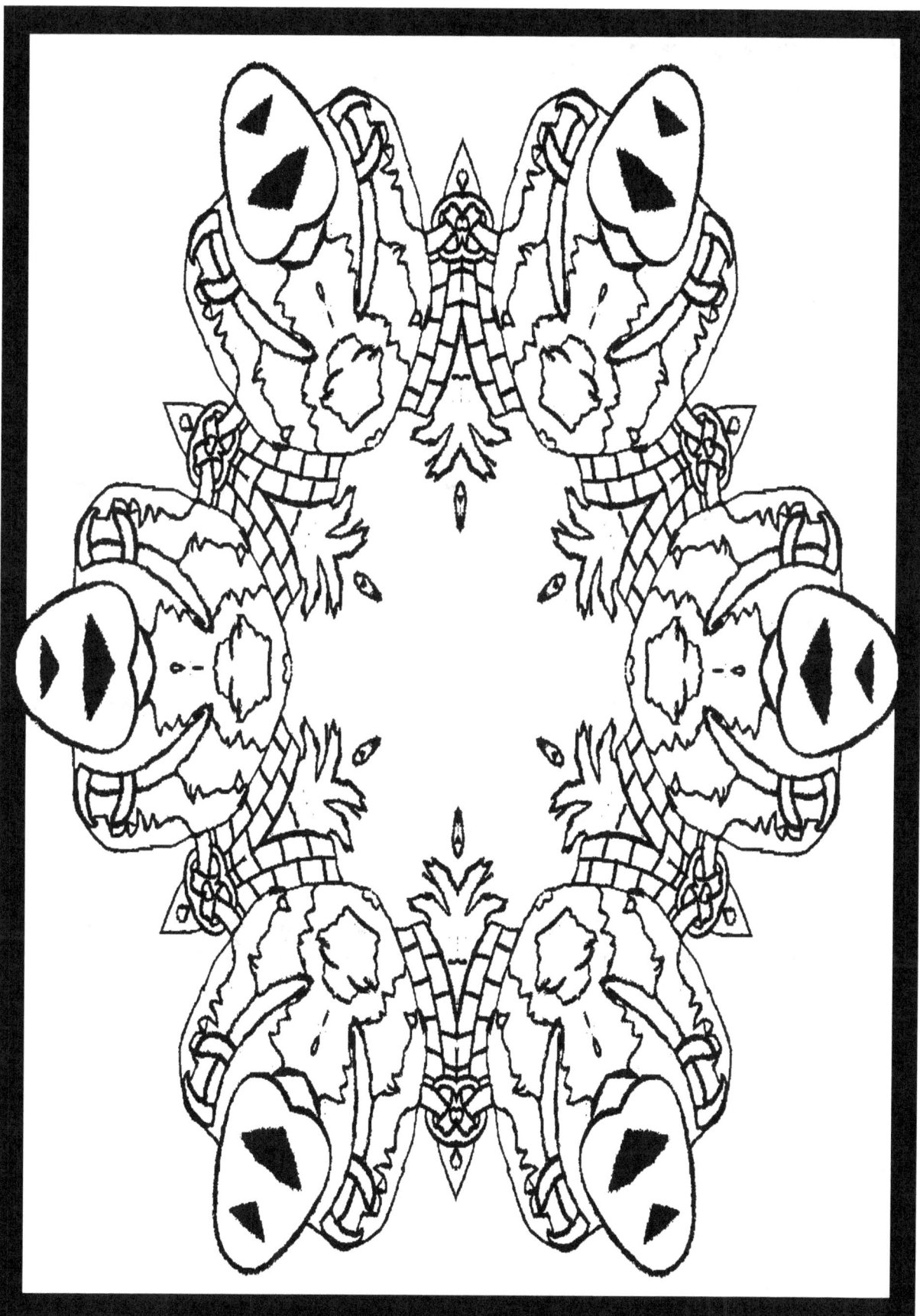

I promise this is the last one now. Special thanks page follows. Hope you enjoyed this book and hope you show it to everyone you know. Thanks again for coloring my work, it means the world to me.

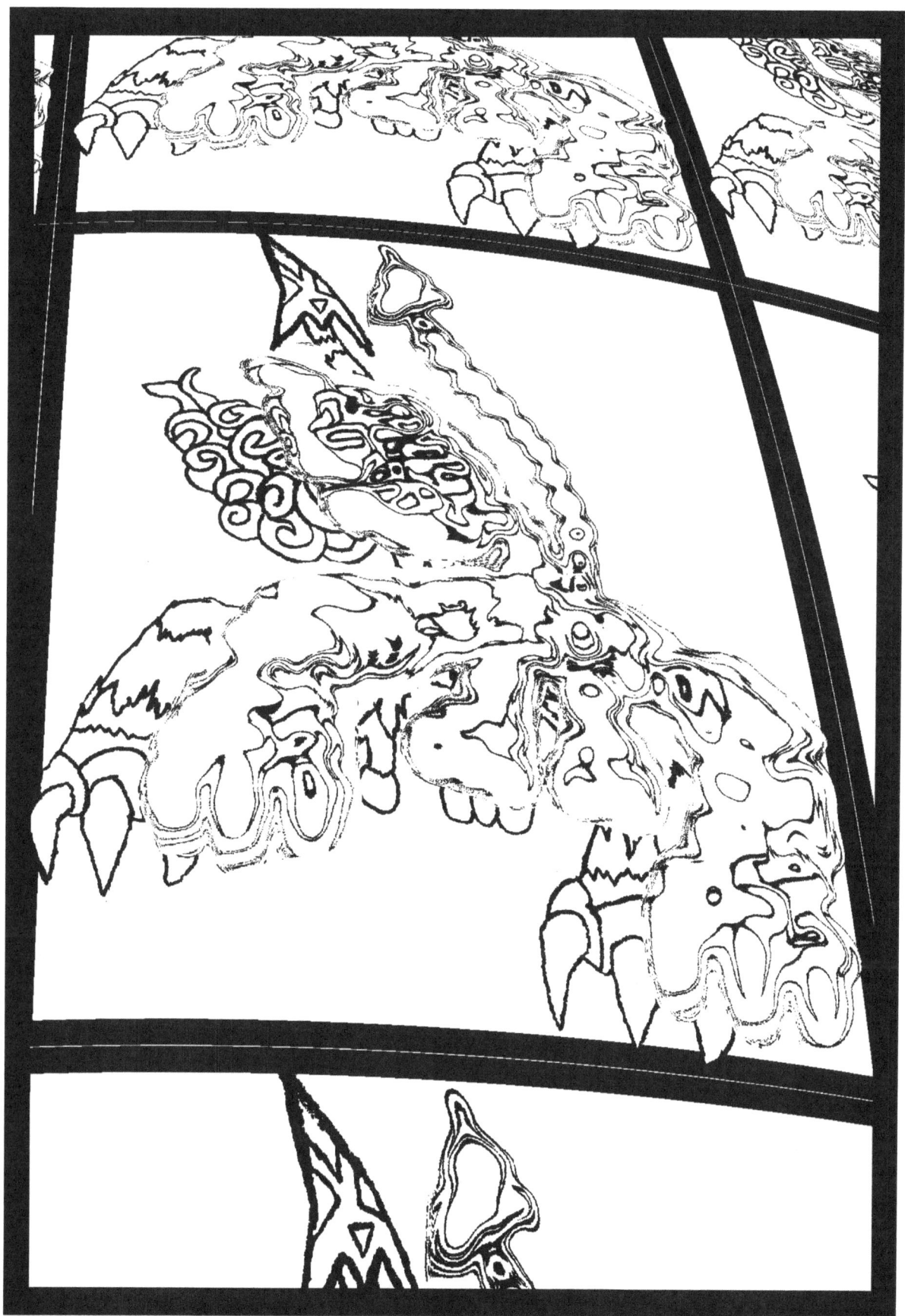

Special Thanks Pages:

As with all my work, I must give credit where credit is due. I'd like to first off thank anyone who has supported me through the years with seeing my artistic potential when I haven't. I would also like to thank anyone who has purchased or enjoyed copies of my first book, <u>Lucid Linework</u>, and inspiring me to move forward with my art. You guys are the best.

Now it's time for the personal shout outs. First I would like to thank my friends, Ian and Lexi, for helping with Lucid Linework with grammar corrections, advertising, and giving me a scanner to allow me to work from home on my books. A special thanks to my buddy, Jeff, for being supportive and patient while I constantly pester him with looking at my drawings. None of this would be possible without my pal, Justin, who aside from teaching me most of what I know about cooking but also helped me find my laptop I am making this on in that dumpster. A shout out to my artist friend and neighbor's dad growing up, Neal, you are one of my key inspirations. I have always enjoyed your art a lot and really did love your coloring book back in the day. Keep up the great work. Have to thank my buddies, Nick and Skokut, for being supportive and friends with me for years.

Most importantly it wouldn't be right to not thank my parents and grandparents for raising me into this world. You guys always put up with me even though I could be a handful at times. Now look though, I am a published author like I always dreamed now and I only plan on moving forward with and building upon these life choices. You guys kick butt.

Seriously though, the most very important thanks are to you, the readers and fans of my work. I really appreciate the support of my dreams and I wish I could share the feeling it gives me with you. It's incredible and my personal advice is if you want to feel it, just follow and fulfill your dreams no matter what. You only have one go at this life so do your best to make it the best. Don't let anything stop you from achieving your dreams, you got this!!!

Once again, thank you to everyone and I apologize if I forgot to mention anybody's names. If I did, contact me and I'll make it right because I surely do appreciate you.